EDITIONS

ARMENIAN
BULGARIAN
BURMESE (Myanmar)
CHINESE
DUTCH
ENGLISH
  Africa
  Australia
  Chinese/English
  India
  Indonesia
  Indonesian/English
  Japan
  Korean/English
  Korean/English/
    Japanese
  Myanmar
  Philippines
  Singapore
  Sri Lanka
  United Kingdom
  United States
ESTONIAN
FRENCH
GREEK
GUJARATI
HINDI
HUNGARIAN
IBAN/ENGLISH
ILOKANO
INDONESIAN
ITALIAN
JAPANESE
KANNADA
KOREAN
MALAYALAM
NEPALI
NORWEGIAN
ODIA
POLISH
PORTUGUESE
  Africa
  Brazil
  Portugal
RUSSIAN
SINHALA
SPANISH
  Caribbean
  Mexico
  South America
  United States
SWEDISH
TAMIL
TELUGU
THAI
URDU

THE UP

WHERE THE WORLD MEETS TO PRAY

Sarah Wilke
Publisher

INTERDENOMINATIONAL
INTERNATIONAL
INTERRACIAL

33 LANGUAGES
Multiple formats are available in some languages

The Upper Room
May–August 2016
Edited by Susan Hibbins

The Upper Room © BRF 2016
The Bible Reading Fellowship
15 The Chambers, Vineyard, Abingdon OX14 3FE
Tel: 01865 319700; Fax: 01865 319701
Email: enquiries@brf.org.uk
Website: www.brf.org.uk
BRF is a Registered Charity

ISBN 978 0 85746 395 1

Acknowledgments

The New Revised Standard Version of the Bible, Anglicized Edition, copyright © 1989, 1995 by the Division of Christian Education of the National Council of the Churches of Christ in the USA. Used by permission. All rights reserved.

The Holy Bible, New International Version, copyright © 1973, 1978, 1984 by International Bible Society. Used by permission of Hodder & Stoughton Publishers, a member of the Hachette Livre UK Group. All rights reserved. 'NIV' is a registered trademark of International Bible Society. UK trademark number 1448790.

Extracts from the Authorised Version of the Bible (The King James Bible), the rights in which are vested in the Crown, are reproduced by permission of the Crown's Patentee, Cambridge University Press.

Scriptures quoted from the Good News Bible published by The Bible Societies/HarperCollins Publishers Ltd, UK © American Bible Society 1966, 1971, 1976, 1992, used by permission.

Extracts from CEB copyright © 2011 by Common English Bible.

Printed by Gutenberg Press, Tarxien, Malta

The Upper Room: how to use this book

The Upper Room is ideal in helping us spend a quiet time with God each day. Each daily entry is based on a passage of scripture, and is followed by a meditation and prayer. Each person who contributes a meditation to the magazine seeks to relate their experience of God in a way that will help those who use The Upper Room every day.

Here are some guidelines to help you make best use of The Upper Room:

1. Read the passage of Scripture. It is a good idea to read it more than once, in order to have a fuller understanding of what it is about and what you can learn from it.
2. Read the meditation. How does it relate to your own experience? Can you identify with what the writer has outlined from their own experience or understanding?
3. Pray the written prayer. Think about how you can use it to relate to people you know, or situations that need your prayers today.
4. Think about the contributor who has written the meditation. Some Upper Room users include this person in their prayers for the day.
5. Meditate on the 'Thought for the Day', the 'Link2Life' and the 'Prayer Focus', perhaps using them again as the focus for prayer or direction for action.

Why is it important to have a daily quiet time? Many people will agree that it is the best way of keeping in touch every day with the God who sustains us, and who sends us out to do his will and show his love to the people we encounter each day. Meeting with God in this way reassures us of his presence with us, helps us to discern his will for us and makes us part of his worldwide family of Christian people through our prayers.

I hope that you will be encouraged as you use the magazine regularly as part of your daily devotions, and that God will richly bless you as you read his word and seek to learn more about him.

Susan Hibbins
UK Editor

In Times of/For Help with . . .

Below is a list of entries in this copy of *The Upper Room* relating to situations or emotions with which we may need help:

Assurance: May 22; June 9
Bible reading/study: May 9; June 12, 24; July 2, 4, 25; Aug 5, 10, 30
Busyness/distractions: May 3
Change: Aug 18
Christian community: June 4, 30
Comfort: June 25; Aug 2, 19
Creation: July 24; 16, Aug 25
Encouragement: May 6, 18, 21; June 22; July 8, 29; Aug 6, 14
Evangelism: May 13, 28; June 14; July 16, 21; Aug 3, 4, 27
Faith: May 23, 26, 27; June 16, 17, 29; July 6, 27; Aug 1, 14, 27
Forgiveness: May 11, 30; June 7, 15; July 24
God's goodness/love/grace: May 2, 3, 29; June 2, 7, 29; July 3, 25
God's presence: May 14, 17; June 23; July 5, 10, Aug. 2, 19, 16
God's provision: May 3, 19; June 4, 9, 27; Aug 12
Gratitude: June 20
Growth: May 20; June 16, 22; July 30; Aug 1
Guidance: May 21, 25; June 24; July 21, 26
Heaven: May 5; June 2; Aug 7
Healing/illness: May 24, 26, 29; July 3, 15; Aug 22
Hope: May 12, 16; June 1, 17, 20, 26, 27
Humility: June 12
Joy: June 2, 9
Judging: May 1; June 8, 25; July 1
Listening/waiting for God: May 2, 4, 24; June 13; July 4, 23; Aug 23, 29, 31
Living our faith: May 6, 8, 10, 18, 31; June 15; July 11; Aug 3, 8

Obedience: May 27; June; Aug 1
Praise: May 7; Aug 16
Parenting: May 20
Peace: May 11; June 5; July 14, 22, 25; Aug 24
Perseverance: July 8
Prayer: May 4, 10, 12, 26; June 1, 17, 30; July 4, 23, 31; Aug 5, 6, 30
Renewal: May 14, 29
Salvation: May 5; June 7, 26; Aug 15
Security: Aug 7
Serving: May 23, 31; June 10, 24; July 6, 27; Aug 4, 9, 10, 20
Spiritual practices: June 29; July 2, 4; Aug 5
Strength: May 20; June 1, 5; July 29; Aug 9, 12
Stress/Worry/Anxiety: May 24; June 13, 28
Trust: May 2, 4, 20; June 2, 16, 27, 29; July 6, 17, 28; Aug 7, 22, 28
Worship: July 7

The Power of Pentecost

When they heard this sound, a crowd came together in bewilderment, because each one heard their own language being spoken. Utterly amazed, they asked: 'Aren't all these who are speaking Galileans? Then how is it that each of us hears them in our native language?' (Acts 2:6–8, NIV).

This 'little book' has close ties to Pentecost, the miraculous moment when the disciples gathered after Christ's ascension in the place called the Upper Room. As the disciples spoke, the Holy Spirit appeared as 'tongues of fire' above their heads. A crowd 'from every nation under heaven' was there to listen, and somehow they were able to hear the words in their own languages.

The power of Pentecost is often depicted in modern church services by recruiting several people who can read a second language. Together, they recite the Acts 2 passage, sometimes with eight or ten languages spoken in unison. The effect is to emphasise the miracle of the speaking in tongues.

But perhaps the real miracle of Pentecost is in the listening. Remember that the disciples were all speaking the same language. The words, though, fell on the ears of the listeners in their native languages, and the Spirit-filled message they heard inspired them to become disciples themselves.

Here at *The Upper Room*, it is our sacred mission to listen, and it has been almost from the start. When the magazine began in 1936, it was filled with devotions written exclusively by 'experts'—clergy, educators, scholars. But soon everyday readers began submitting stories of their own personal encounters with the Holy Spirit. Our early leaders had the wisdom to embrace these precious stories; and within three years, *The Upper Room* became a publication that depended completely on its reader-writers.

As these Spirit-filled stories continue to arrive each day, we listen—and we share them with joy. Combined, these individual voices in many different tongues have drawn together a faithful community of millions around the world.

Sarah Wilke, Publisher

Where the World Meets to Pray

The first edition of *The Upper Room* in the Thai language was printed in 1953. The Reverend Kenneth E. Wells served as the editor in Thailand. The new publication marked a significant step forward in developing a programme of Christian education in this country. Since the first issue, the development of Christian literature and resources in Thailand has continued to grow. Over the past 60 years the number of copies has increased with each printing of *The Upper Room*, and today the circulation of the magazine is about 6,500 copies per issue.

We give thanks to God that the Thai language edition has helped Thai people know God and has helped Christians gain a deeper experience of faith. With the help of the magazine, people in Thailand have the opportunity for a closer relationship with God individually, in their family life, in churches, in schools, and in hospitals.

We are happy to belong to *The Upper Room* family. In Thailand, as it is everywhere around the globe, *The Upper Room* is where the world meets to pray.

Reverend Prasartporn Tariyo
Editor, Thai language edition of The Upper Room

The Editor writes...

Recently I was reading the passage in John's Gospel in which Jesus meets the men who would become his disciples for the first time (John 1:35–49). Previously they had been the disciples of John the Baptist, who had baptised Jesus the day before; now John encourages his followers to go to Jesus instead, and two of them ask Jesus where he is staying. Jesus replies, 'Come and see', and they spend the rest of the day with him.

Andrew, one of the disciples, fetches his brother Simon, telling him they have found the Messiah. The next day, in Galilee, Jesus calls Philip to follow him; Philip then goes to find his friend Nathanael to tell him about Jesus. To Nathanael's doubtful reaction Philip responds, echoing Jesus, 'Come and see.'

To me this story seems a very simple and early example of the spread of Jesus' message to the world. The disciples who had spent even a little time with Jesus wanted their friends to have the same experience: to know Jesus. If we have experience of Jesus' saving grace in our lives today, do we not want to do the same?

And what of other people we meet? How do we respond to someone who has no knowledge of Jesus, or of the Christian life? Do we suggest they start reading the Bible? Should we try theological argument? Talking about creation, can we argue for the existence of God? Do we point out the ten commandments or the importance of tithing? Which church service should we invite people to attend?

All these options will have a part to play. But Jesus' first invitation was 'Come and see.' By our lives, our actions, our words and our love for each other, we too can say, 'Come and see', and help others to begin a living, transforming friendship with Jesus.

Susan Hibbins
Editor of the UK edition

The Bible readings are selected with great care, and we urge you to include the suggested reading in your devotional time.

SUNDAY 1 MAY

Peace of Jesus

Read Matthew 7:1–12

When pride comes, then comes disgrace, but with humility comes wisdom.
Proverbs 11:2 (NIV)

My job required me to run long computer reports for the engineering department. One day, the programming department asked me to stop running the reports in order to run their software tests. Even though I was behind schedule, I did so. But the software tests kept failing. The programmers kept modifying the software, which then required more testing.

My patience waned and I became angry. I felt that resources were being wasted. Instead of asking if their tests could be run later, I belittled the programmers in front of other people. I thought my critical statements made me look important, but later I realised that they only made me look foolish. Angry and judgemental, I had forgotten the Golden Rule: 'In everything, do to others what you would have them do to you' (Matthew 7:12).

My pride and impatience blinded my judgement. I now wish I could take back my actions from that day. Criticising others for a fault while remaining blind to my own considerable fault is hypocritical. Jesus taught, 'Do not judge and you will not be judged. Do not condemn and you will not be condemned. Forgive and you will be forgiven' (Luke 6:37). After much soul searching and Bible study, I now know that God is gracious to me and calls me to be gracious to others.

Prayer: *Gracious God, thank you for your steadfast grace. Help us to remain on a path of humility and love. Amen*

Thought for the day: God does not hold my sins against me.

Les Brisbois (Arizona, US)

PRAYER FOCUS: SOMEONE STRUGGLING WITH PATIENCE

MONDAY 2 MAY

Are You Listening?

Read John 10:1–18

[The shepherd] calls his own sheep by name and leads them out. When he has brought out all his own, he goes on ahead of them, and his sheep follow him because they know his voice.
John 10:3–4 (NIV)

My 14-year-old miniature dachshund is blind. I am constantly amazed that she can still go anywhere she wants. Sometimes, though, she bumps into things and gets confused. When that happens, I call her name, urging her to come to me. Hearing my voice, she turns her head, perks up her ears and redirects herself. She trusts me to lead her to her destination safely. Because she recognises my voice, she follows obediently.

When I see my dog's response to my call, I wonder about how often I fail to hear God calling me amid the busyness of my day. Do I listen for God when I bump into things and get confused? Do I follow his call? I don't do as well at hearing and obeying God as my dog does me. However, I am trying to be more aware of his call, becoming more obedient and following where he leads.

Even more than we care about pets and others whom we love, God cares about and loves us. Our part is to pray and read God's word—listening for his voice and striving to follow his way.

Prayer: *Dear God, open our ears so that we may clearly hear your call and go where you are calling us. Amen*

Thought for the day: How can I better hear God's voice and learn to be more obedient?

Virgilia Moore (North Carolina, US)

PRAYER FOCUS: THOSE WHO HAVE IMPAIRED VISION

TUESDAY 3 MAY

Count Your Blessings

Read Matthew 6:25–33

It is as if the dew of Hermon were falling on Mount Zion. For there the Lord bestows his blessing, even life for evermore.
Psalm 133:3 (NIV)

Early one September, I was spending a couple of days in my cabin in the forest. The cranberries were ripe, and I had planned to pick some to make cranberry jelly. As I went along the path leading away from my cabin, I had to look very carefully to see the red berries. Then they seemed to appear suddenly, and I picked as many as I could find. But later, when I returned to the cabin along the same path, I discovered many berries left for me still to pick—berries I hadn't seen the first time.

Life can seem like my journey along the forest path. As we hurry along the roads of life, we occasionally stop to enjoy the blessings that God bestows on us before we hurry on again. But when we stop hurrying and make an effort to search for God's blessings, he can open our eyes to see even more blessings and love.

The busyness of life sometimes distracts us from seeing the love of God clearly. But when we stop to spend time in prayer and meditation, God reveals far beyond what we may see at first glance.

Prayer: *Dear Lord, thank you for loving us with an everlasting love. Keep us close to you even when we are not able to see your blessings. We pray in Jesus' name. Amen*

Thought for the day: God offers blessings beyond what we can see or imagine.

Øystein Brinch (Oslo, Norway)

PRAYER FOCUS: SOMEONE STRUGGLING WITH DEPRESSION

WEDNESDAY 4 MAY

Waiting for God

Read Psalm 13:1–6
Wait for the Lord; be strong, and let your heart take courage; wait for the Lord!
Psalm 27:14 (NRSV)

Recently one of my close friends described the way in which God had quickly answered her prayer. After hearing about her experience, I found myself not glad for her, but jealous. For over a year now I had searched for a new job without success. I couldn't understand why God was not quicker to help me in my current situation. Why did my friend have a quick answer, while I had to wait for God to act?

After seeking answers in my Bible, I realised that many people before me had waited. David waited years to become king. The people of Israel waited for generations to find their promised land. Joseph and Mary waited to see how their son would save his people. The disciples waited following the crucifixion of Jesus to find out what was happening—what the true outcome of Jesus' death would be.

God still calls us to wait. We do not know the what, where or why of how God works; but Romans 8:28 tells us that 'all things work together for good for those who love God'—even if it takes longer than we'd like!

Prayer: *O Lord, we pray that you will give us an attitude of peace and gratitude for the blessings you have shown us. Give us strength to wait for you even in the toughest of situations. Amen*

Thought for the day: While I wait, I will trust in God.

Sue A. Fairchild (Pennsylvania, US)

PRAYER FOCUS: PEOPLE WAITING FOR ANSWERS FROM GOD

THURSDAY 5 MAY

Journey Home

Read Hebrews 11:8–16

They are seeking a homeland… they desire a better country, that is, a heavenly one. Therefore God is not ashamed to be called their God; indeed, he has prepared a city for them.
Hebrews 11:14, 16 (NRSV)

I am 'Omo Ogbomoso'—a child of Ogbomoso—born in a mission guest house in Nigeria. My family left my childhood home for America when I was twelve, and I thought I would never return. Imagine my joy when I had the opportunity to visit nearly 40 years later.

The house I grew up in was still there, and I introduced myself to the Nigerians who lived there. They invited me inside. How amazing to walk through the house, looking at rooms where I used to play!

There's a phrase that describes people like me: 'Third Culture Kids' (TCKs). To us, the term 'home' gets confusing. Is home America? Or is it Africa? Or is it a mixture? Home is Arkansas, my mother's home, where we lived when on leave from the mission field. Home is also Missouri, where I visited Dad's parents, and Texas, where I've lived most of my adult life. And home is also a city half a world away.

Today's reading explains that all believers are TCKs; we are all searching for our home—our heavenly one. Imagine our joy when we finally reach it and are united with Christ.

Prayer: *Heavenly Father, thank you that by your grace, we will someday be in our heavenly home. In Jesus' name we pray. Amen*

Thought for the day: How will my life today reflect my longing for God's heavenly home?

Ron Wasson (Texas, US)

PRAYER FOCUS: CHILDREN OF MISSIONARIES

FRIDAY 6 MAY

Let Your Light Shine

Read Matthew 5:13–16
You are the light of the world. A city built on a hill cannot be hid… let your light shine before others, so that they may see your good works and give glory to your Father in heaven.
Matthew 5:14, 16 (NRSV)

When I visited an area known for fireflies recently, the leader of the group led us down a pathway to the river in total darkness. Silently we got into a boat, and the oarsman rowed us downstream. As we floated past the bushes growing on the banks of the river, we were delighted to see clouds of fireflies lifting up into the darkness. They performed a pirouette and then resettled in the next bush. The fireflies repeated this display all the way down the river—brightening each area for a few seconds.

In today's reading, Jesus reminds us that, like those fireflies, we are called to let our light shine in the world and into the lives of others. When we encounter someone who feels depressed or discouraged or who has lost hope, we have an opportunity to share the light of Christ's love.

Prayer: *God of Light, fill us with your love so that we may brighten the way for those who stumble in darkness. We pray as Jesus taught us, saying, 'Our Father which art in heaven, Hallowed be thy name. Thy kingdom come. Thy will be done, as in heaven, so in earth. Give us day by day our daily bread. And forgive us our sins; for we also forgive every one that is indebted to us. And lead us not into temptation; but deliver us from evil.'* Amen*

Thought for the day: To whom can I bring God's light today?

Winifred Montgomery (Gauteng, South Africa)

PRAYER FOCUS: SOMEONE WHO NEEDS MY ENCOURAGEMENT
* Luke 11:2–4, KJV

SATURDAY 7 MAY

Magnify the Lord

Read Psalm 34:1–10

O magnify the Lord with me and let us exalt his name together!
Psalm 34:3 (NRSV)

As a teenager I regularly attended my church's Wednesday night prayer meeting. Each week during the sharing time an elderly man, Mr Hamel, would invariably stand to his feet and with a confident voice recite Psalm 34:3, 'O magnify the Lord with me and let us exalt his name together!' Then he would share an experience from the past week that attested to God's faithfulness and goodness. He did not request prayer regarding his needs or problems; his focus was solely on God's magnificence.

Sometimes our problems can seem insurmountable. And they may be, if we rely on our strength alone. But the God who promises to sustain and deliver us is greater than the trials that beset us. When we stop focusing on our difficulties and view our present circumstances through the word of God, the magnitude of our problems will diminish and the magnificence of our God will become apparent. Then, even during the trials of life, we can testify to God's goodness and faithfulness.

Prayer: *Almighty God, help us remember your power and love and to praise you in every situation. Amen*

Thought for the day: Today I will focus on God's magnificence.

Wayne Greenawalt (Illinois, US)

PRAYER FOCUS: SOMEONE WHOSE FAITH INSPIRES ME

SUNDAY 8 MAY

Brothers and Sisters

Read Acts 28:11–16

At the sight of [the brothers and sisters] Paul thanked God and was encouraged.
Acts 28:15 (NIV)

As a family we had wonderful outings on our bicycles, at a time when there were few cars on the road. My brother John was the eldest and so he liked to be out in front. We still laugh at the time when we thought he must have reached our destination; we saw him, head down, cycling towards us, oblivious of the fact that he had come full circle round a roundabout by mistake.

But there were other times when I would be struggling uphill when, from behind, a strong hand was planted in the middle of my back and I felt myself pushed upwards. My brother had willingly given up his lead to come back and help his little sister.

As I have recently joined with my family in thanksgiving for my brother's well-lived life, I have thought how important it is that we love and care for one another. The great apostle Paul was encouraged by those who stood at the roadside to support him as he was led as a prisoner toward Rome, and David, who would become a mighty king, was strengthened by the help and friendship of Jonathan. As my brother helped me, we can help our Christian brothers and sisters when they are struggling.

Prayer: *Thank you, Lord, for those who help us on our journey; help us to do the same for others. Amen*

Thought for the day: We can all encourage others by showing that we care.

Pauline Lewis (South Wales, UK)

PRAYER FOCUS: FAMILIES

MONDAY 9 MAY

The Best Part of the Day

Read Romans 10:5–13

All scripture is inspired by God and is useful for teaching, for reproof, for correction, and for training in righteousness, so that everyone who belongs to God may be proficient, equipped for every good work.
2 Timothy 3:16–17 (NRSV)

I have often heard people say that they like to read their Bible early in the morning because it shapes their minds and actions throughout the day. I have not always practised this habit, but now I feel compelled to reach for my Bible and my copy of *The Upper Room* as soon as I awaken. Before I begin my reading, I pray the prayer below. I anticipate this practice with great joy; it is the best part of the day.

When my Bible was new many years ago, I didn't write in it because I wanted it to retain its newness. Now my Bible is worn and contains many notes in the margins. I frequently underline sentences and paragraphs that are especially meaningful to me. When I come across those highlighted words, I read them and feel God speaking to me again.

Someday, when I am no longer here, my sons or grandchildren may find my Bible and read the words that I have marked, gaining insight into God's special love for them. They may even hear his voice speaking to them. In this way I hope that my love for God's word will be an example to them, even after my earthly life is done.

Prayer: *Dear Lord, open my heart and my mind to the power of your word so that, as I read, I may know, understand and obey what you say to me today. In Jesus' name. Amen*

Thought for the day: Today I will spend time with God.

Lynn Moran (Alabama, US)

PRAYER FOCUS: THOSE WHO DO NOT HAVE ACCESS TO BIBLES

TUESDAY 10 MAY

Counting On God

Read Psalm 52:8–9
The Lord is good; his steadfast love endures for ever, and his faithfulness to all generations.
Psalm 100:5 (NRSV)

I went to the front door to get the newspaper, which is delivered to my home every morning at 5:30. I took the paper from the letterbox and returned to the kitchen, where I remarked, 'You can always count on the papergirl.'

My wife responded, 'That is the best thing you can say about anyone.'

We can especially count on God to be with us and to be willing to listen and to consider our prayers. We do not have to wonder and worry about the reaction we will receive as we speak our thoughts and cares to him. When we need help, he is always available.

From God, we learn how to be peaceful listeners by taking the time to listen more and to talk less. God gives us the strength to focus on meaningful conversations. He is the best example of a good listener, available and approachable, the One on whom we can all rely. God is accessible from anywhere in the world.

Prayer: *Dear God, thank you for always being ready to listen. Help us to listen carefully to you and to others. Amen*

Thought for the day: I can always count on God.

Michael W. Johnson (Montana, US)

PRAYER FOCUS: TO BE A DEPENDABLE LISTENER

WEDNESDAY 11 MAY

Forgiveness

Read Luke 6:35–38

Be tolerant with each other and, if someone has a complaint against anyone, forgive each other. As the Lord forgave you, so also forgive each other.
Colossians 3:13 (CEB)

Ten years ago in Baudó, Colombia, a family friend took the life of my father. My family had helped this person, along with some of his other family members. After a falling out with my brother, this person sought revenge by killing my father. His senseless act filled me with unbelievable hatred for him.

Later, I visited the city of Cali where my aunt lived and she invited me to her church. As I learned more about Jesus Christ I accepted him as my Saviour and my faith increased. I also attended prayer meetings held at my aunt's house. At one such meeting, the leader led us in prayer based on the theme of forgiveness. At that moment I sensed a very real presence persuading me that in order to seek forgiveness from God, I first had to forgive my father's killer.

After we had prayed, the leader asked each person to share any comments about our prayer time. When it was my turn, I opened my mouth but could not speak. I wept as I was overcome by the marvellous transformation I had just experienced. Since then, I have gained inner peace and am at peace with other people. I have learned to pray for the person who caused my family harm. We can all experience the salvation and forgiveness that God offers.

Prayer: *Loving God, help us to forgive others as you have forgiven us. Amen*

Thought for the day: With God's help I can forgive and love anyone.

Sindy Yuliana Granja (Cali, Colombia)

PRAYER FOCUS: FOR THE COURAGE TO FORGIVE

THURSDAY 12 MAY

The Blackbird's Song

Read Psalm 57:7–8
Faith is confidence in what we hope for and assurance about what we do not see.
Hebrews 11:1 (NIV)

When I participated in an all-night prayer vigil for a dear friend with cancer, one of my prayer slots was at four in the morning—not a time when I am at my best. It was still dark when I rose to pray. All was quiet outside. As I attempted to rouse myself to intercede for my friend, a rich and joyful sound burst into the darkness. It was a blackbird, perched on the roof of my neighbour's house. Its beautiful song split the darkness with joy and exuberance in anticipation of the dawn.

Hearing the bird's song—even before the sunrise—caused my mind to turn to the well-known verse in Hebrews 11:1: 'Faith is confidence in what we hope for and assurance about what we do not see.' I returned to my prayer time with renewed hope and anticipation of God's help and support for my friend. I knew that as surely as the dawn broke, our God would be merciful and faithful to her. I joined in a song of praise with my little blackbird friend, causing steadfastness and hope to rise in my own soul. Our faith can awaken with the dawn of each new day.

Prayer: *Dear God, give hope to all who wait for a new and better day. Reassure us of your faithfulness. Amen*

Thought for the day: I can praise God for all the wonders I am about to see.

Janice Ross (Scotland)

PRAYER FOCUS: THOSE STRUGGLING WITH CANCER

FRIDAY 13 MAY

Ripples

Read 1 Corinthians 15:1–11

Go ye therefore, and teach all nations, baptising them in the name of the Father, and of the Son, and of the Holy Ghost.
Matthew 28:19 (KJV)

When my son Justin was about five, I took him fishing with me. He put on his waders and hat and brought along his little fishing rod. When we got to the lake, we set up camp and put our lines in the water. We were ready for a long day of fishing. After ten or fifteen minutes, however, Justin got bored, picked up some stones and threw them into the water. Then he watched the ripples spread in all directions.

As Christians, we are like the ripples in the lake. When we read scripture and follow its guidance, we can go out in all directions and tell other people about God's love and saving grace. When they receive the message, they go out and tell more people about the word of God. Those, in turn, tell more people. The motion occurs naturally, like ripples on the lake.

Jesus said, 'Go ye therefore, and teach all nations, baptising them in the name of the Father, and of the Son, and of the Holy Ghost' (Matthew 28:19). He was telling us to be ripples and to go out and make more ripples, who go out and make even more ripples. What a wonderful idea!

Prayer: *Dear God, give us every chance to bring people to you so that they, in turn, can make more ripples. Amen*

Thought for the day: The word of God spreads out like ripples on water.

Andrew Mills (Pennsylvania, US)

PRAYER FOCUS: TO SHARE CHRIST WITH OTHERS

SATURDAY 14 MAY

Rebuilding Our Faith

Read Malachi 3:6–12

I have loved you, says the Lord; but you say, 'How have you loved us?'
Malachi 1:2 (CEB)

Bills and paperwork for my struggling business were strewn around my cramped living room. I couldn't help but wonder if my surroundings were the ruins of a failed life, the evidence of unmet expectations. 'Is God disappointed in me?' I wondered. 'If not, where is God in this moment?'

After their release from captivity in Babylon, the Israelites asked the same questions as they gazed over the ruins of their lives in Jerusalem. God answered with an assurance both simple and profound: 'I have loved you' (Malachi 1:2). God wasn't concerned by the crumbling walls or the need to make up for lost time. Rather, God wanted the people to know of his love; he has loved them in the past and he loves them now.

The answer is the same for us. God loves us exactly where we are today. What we may see as ruins, he sees as building blocks for lives greater than we could imagine for ourselves. As we shift our focus from our messy surroundings to God's presence, he will redeem and rebuild our lives.

Prayer: *Thank you, Lord, for your unfailing love and closeness, no matter where we are in life. Amen*

Thought for the day: In the midst of my troubles, where can I sense God's presence?

Megan L. Anderson (Indiana, US)

PRAYER FOCUS: SMALL-BUSINESS OWNERS

SUNDAY 15 MAY

An Interfaith Experience

Read Psalm 100:1–5

How good and pleasant it is when kindred live together in unity!
Psalm 133:1 (NRSV)

The rabbi of a nearby Jewish synagogue invited our choir to sing with theirs for an upcoming community service. After the service was over, I asked the choir conductor if I might join her choir even though I am not of the Jewish faith. The conductor spoke to the rabbi, who said he would be happy for me to become a choir member. I was thrilled to be able to sing with them but even more excited to learn about the Hebrew language and their faith.

On Christmas Eve, a man from the synagogue visited my church. The next time we saw each other, I was singing in the Shabbat evening service. He approached me, asking if he might join my church's choir. He did join us, receiving a warm welcome from the choir members and the conductor.

Experiences like my three years of singing with my Jewish friend can give us new eyes to see each other as people of value. Learning about each other's traditions and faith can change and enrich our lives. God's love and grace enable us to reach across divides and learn about other faiths, while also strengthening our own.

Prayer: *Dear God, thank you for valuable and enriching experiences that teach us to love our brothers and sisters of different faiths. Amen*

Thought for the day: Learning about different faiths can enrich my own.

Sally McGinley (Pennsylvania, US)

PRAYER FOCUS: LEARNING TO ACCEPT PEOPLE OF DIFFERENT FAITHS

MONDAY 16 MAY

God's Maths

Read Matthew 14:13–21

Is anything too hard for the Lord?
Genesis 18:14 (NIV)

Five years ago, when I was still a university student, I had a problem with an assignment from my professor. My assignment was due the next afternoon, and I had no time to fix its many mistakes. I was stressed.

The next afternoon, when I was working my job as a tutor, one of my students asked me, 'Can you give me the answer to a question? How many is five plus two?'

His question made me angry because he was quite capable of answering the question by himself. I answered him, 'You know the answer is seven. Why are you asking me?'

With a smile, he replied, 'No, in your maths, five plus two is seven, but not in God's maths. For him, five plus two is more than five thousand because he can feed five thousand people with only five loaves of bread and two fish.'

His question and answer relieved my stress and made me calm. Reflecting on this, I prayed for God's help, and to my surprise, my professor gave me one more week to finish my assignment. Now, I remember that God is always present with us, bringing hope and peace.

Prayer: *Beloved God, help us to realise that you never forsake us. In all circumstances, our help comes from you. Amen*

Thought for the day: 'All things are possible for God' (Matthew 19:26, CEB).

Linawati Santoso (East Java, Indonesia)

PRAYER FOCUS: PRIMARY SCHOOL PUPILS

TUESDAY 17 MAY

Simply There

Read Job 14:1–14

A person's days are determined; you have decreed the number of his months and have set limits he cannot exceed.
Job 14:5 (NIV)

My nephew is now healthy and energetic, but that was not always the case. When he was born, the hospital staff quickly took him to the neo-natal intensive care unit to resolve some complications that the doctor assured my brother and sister-in-law were minor. That assurance did not stop our family from experiencing anxiety and doubt. I felt helpless and worried that my minutes'-old nephew had reached his 'determined days' before they had even begun.

I asked my mother, an experienced nurse, and Dad—a pastor—if we could do anything to help. I also asked God how something like this could happen. Mum said, 'I cannot do much, but I am praying simply that God will be with him and with the doctors.' Dad responded, with tears in his eyes, 'Sometimes praying is all we can do.' I felt powerless and empty, but in that moment, I did not feel alone.

I think my initial loneliness that day was similar to the overwhelming fear and isolation Christians experience on Holy Saturday. The coming resurrection offers hope, but future hope often does not change present grief. God was present in the days between Jesus' death and resurrection, just as he continues to be with all of us during difficult days. Though the words of Job 14 haunt me, I can take refuge in the God who is always there.

Prayer: *Dear God, you are with us always. Help us live in a way that reflects your eternal presence. Amen*

Thought for the day: When praying is all we can do, that is enough.

Jonathan Redding (Tennessee, US)

PRAYER FOCUS: STAFF OF INTENSIVE CARE UNITS

WEDNESDAY 18 MAY

The Words of our Mouths

Read James 3:1–12
From the same mouth come blessing and cursing. My brothers and sisters, this ought not to be so.
James 3:10 (NRSV)

As a child, I struggled with reading and spelling—until I met an understanding teacher, Mrs G. Just before a spelling test one day, she pulled me aside. 'I wonder if you would be more comfortable spelling your words out loud while you help me decorate this notice board.'

A few minutes later she said, 'You've answered them all correctly, even the ones you weren't supposed to know!' Always a poor student, I was amazed. Had I really done that well?

Mrs G's compassion and sensitivity encouraged me and showed me I could succeed. In many ways she told me that she believed in me when I couldn't believe in myself. No wonder the Bible reminds us that our words have the power to bless as well as curse! My life was truly blessed by my teacher's loving words.

With God's help each of us can live out Psalm 19:14: 'Let the words of my mouth and the meditation of my heart be acceptable to you, O Lord, my rock and my redeemer.'

Prayer: *Help us, O God, to speak words of kindness and compassion. Make us sensitive to those who need to hear your love from our lips. In Jesus' name. Amen*

Thought for the day: 'Anxiety weighs down the heart, but a kind word cheers it up' (Proverbs 12:25, NIV).

Ramona Furst (Ontario, Canada)

PRAYER FOCUS: PUPILS WHO STRUGGLE WITH DYSLEXIA

THURSDAY 19 MAY

Before We Call

Read Isaiah 65:17–25

Before they call I will answer; while they are still speaking I will hear.
Isaiah 65:24 (NIV)

My mind was reviewing the jobs I wanted to do before my baby woke up from her nap. I knew that when she woke up, her nappy would need changing and she would want to be fed. The only way she could tell me about her needs would begin with restlessness and progress to crying.

I was watching the time as I worked, intently listening for her to stir. When that happened, I would hurry to her room before her cries turned into wails. After changing her nappy, I would hold and feed her. I loved my baby and would do anything for her. But while blissfully sleeping, my daughter was in her own little world—unaware of my presence.

As I continued my work, I realised how often I am like my daughter—living in my own little world until what I consider a crisis happens. Then I become frantic and begin wailing to God about my needs and concerns. Yet God's ear is already attuned to our crying and our needs. He is ready to assist us, whatever the problem, even before we call. Thanks be to God for hearing and caring for all of us!

Prayer: *Dear God, thank you for your love that tunes in to our needs even before we know what they are. Amen*

Thought for the day: Even before we call, God is ready and willing to help us.

Donna Trimm (Virginia, US)

PRAYER FOCUS: PARENTS OF YOUNG CHILDREN

FRIDAY 20 MAY

Trusting God

Read Romans 8:28–31

'I know the plans I have for you,' declares the Lord, 'plans to prosper you and not to harm you, plans to give you hope and a future.'
Jeremiah 29:11 (NIV)

I once worked as a department manager in a supermarket. I became frustrated with my job and dismayed that I was not receiving meaningful recognition for my work. As a result of this experience, I thought God might have been testing my faith to see if I would stand firm, building my faith to help me be stronger, or removing something that would harm me or limit my growth in the future.

At times it is difficult to understand what God is doing in our lives. We may ask, 'Why is this happening to me?' On the other hand, we can say, 'I don't know why this is happening, but I know I can trust God to give me what is best.' This is what I chose to do.

Now as I look back and think about how my life has turned out, I see God's hand in the situation and realise that he has been with me and guided me throughout my life.

Such experiences are not pleasant, but God can use them to build our faith and make us stronger. Although we may not understand what he is doing in our lives, God is always faithful and wants what is best for us.

Prayer: *Faithful God, build our faith and our trust in you. Amen*

Thought for the day: God always wants what is best for me.

Paul E. Vander Wege (Iowa, US)

PRAYER FOCUS: SOMEONE SEEKING A NEW JOB

SATURDAY 21 MAY

Store Up God's Word

Read Job 22:21–28

Moses said, 'Keep these words that I am commanding you today in your heart.'
Deuteronomy 6:6 (NRSV)

When I married into a farming family, my responsibilities included bottling, freezing and pickling some of our abundant harvest. I learned to preserve corn, beans, tomatoes and other garden vegetables and luscious fruits. This was a lot to learn—and a lot of work! But I kept at it. Later, the good food I had stored up provided our winter meals, and we enjoyed pickles and fruit jams all year long.

In the same way, if we store up some of the bounty of God's word in our hearts, we can draw sustenance from that supply of encouragement and guidance when lean times come. In prosperous seasons, recalling a challenging Bible verse can jolt us out of spiritual complacency, like a tart bite of pickle. At any time, a scriptural reminder of the Lord's love tastes as sweet as strawberry jam!

Memorising scripture is hard work for me, but I intend to keep at it, to transform my heart into a storehouse of God's word so that I'll always have a rich supply of wisdom and love to see me through!

Prayer: *O God, help us to memorise your word and bring these verses to our minds in times of trouble. As Jesus taught us, we pray, 'Our Father in heaven, hallowed be your name, your kingdom come, your will be done on earth as it is in heaven. Give us today our daily bread. Forgive us our debts, as we also have forgiven our debtors. And lead us not into temptation, but deliver us from the evil one.'* Amen*

Thought for the day: Which words from scripture do I store in my heart?

Linda Bonney Olin (New York, US)

PRAYER FOCUS: FARMERS
* Matthew 6:9–13 (NIV)

SUNDAY 22 MAY

Leftovers or New Beginnings?

Read Acts 9:19–28

If anyone is in Christ, there is a new creation: everything old has passed away; see, everything has become new!
2 Corinthians 5:17 (NRSV)

A few years ago, my church bought a group of caterpillars and placed them in a large netted enclosure in the church. Each caterpillar formed its chrysalis and began emerging from its cocoon two weeks later. One Sunday morning, I caught one glimpse of the net and gulped. 'What has happened?' I wondered. The new butterflies were fluttering around the enclosure, but red splotches that looked like blood stained the netting. Later, I learned that the red substance was actually the leftovers from the butterflies' emergence from the chrysalis. The butterflies were unfolding their beautiful wings, but I couldn't see past their messy leftovers.

The early apostles behaved in a similar way. When Paul, their former persecutor, came to Jerusalem, they were too afraid to meet him. They couldn't look beyond Paul's dark past to see the passionate preacher God was moulding him to be.

God doesn't care about what background we come from; he accepts everyone. Yet, too often, we reject new believers because of their past mistakes. God wants us to look beyond their messy-looking leftovers to the beautiful creations they are becoming through the touch of his loving hands.

Prayer: *O God, help us learn to see others through your eyes. Teach us to see them for the wonderful people you are moulding them—and us—to be. Amen*

Thought for the day: God doesn't care where we've been—only where we are going.

Ruth Anne Burrell (Kansas, US)

PRAYER FOCUS: NEW BELIEVERS

MONDAY 23 MAY

God's Possibilities

Read Matthew 17:14–21
Jesus looked at them and said, 'With man this is impossible, but with God all things are possible.'
Matthew 19:26 (NIV)

I am part of a small ministry based in the United States that raises funds to do work in Guatemala, and our board recently returned from a week-long mission trip there. Unlike many other missions, where work is done by groups travelling from the US, the work that we fund is done by Guatemalan young people. In an area beset by poverty and crime, involving young people is a great way for this ministry to thrive. Coupled with what they learn from weekly Bible studies, they have found that by serving others with these projects, they are serving Christ. Over the six years that we have been in existence, we have seen a big increase in the number of young people who are active within the ministry.

As we were having dinner one night on the trip, I asked our founder if she had expected the growing impact of the ministry when it first started. 'Not at all,' she said, 'but God did.'

We often limit our vision to what we believe is possible. But God's realm of possibility is very different from ours. I know that God will not grant us everything we ask for, but I have seen him respond to people who ask with faith. No request is too big; all things are possible with God.

Prayer: *Dear God, thank you for listening when we ask for your help. Help us to serve others as a way of serving you. Amen*

Thought for the day: No prayer request is too big or too small for God.

John Bown (Minnesota, US)

PRAYER FOCUS: INTERNATIONAL MINISTRIES

TUESDAY 24 MAY

God Does Not Panic

Read Philippians 1:3-11

He who began a good work in you will carry it on to completion until the day of Christ Jesus.
Philippians 1:6 (NIV)

My cousin Brooke had been in perfect health all of her 35 years until one day when she unexpectedly stopped breathing. After resuscitating her, the doctors at the hospital sent her home to await test results. Then, while I was visiting her the symptoms returned. I tried not to show my anxiety and fear as I sat with Brooke and decided whether it was time to call another ambulance.

Suddenly, two little words popped into my head: 'unresting, unhasting'. I recognised them from the second stanza of the hymn, 'Immortal, Invisible, God Only Wise': 'Unresting, unhasting, and silent as light; nor wanting, nor wasting, thou rulest in might.'* These words reminded me that God does not panic. He neither rests nor hurries but is always present and working in our lives. I had to make a quick decision, but in that moment I was able to remain calm, trusting that God was present with us.

Eventually, Brooke received diagnosis and treatment for a rare oesophageal condition. But those two words, 'unresting, unhasting', have stuck with me. I am comforted when I remember that God is continually at work in our lives. Of course, we aren't guaranteed any particular outcome, but we can be confident even during uncertain times that God works on.

Prayer: *Dear God, help us to relax in the knowledge that you neither rest nor hurry as you work in our lives. Amen*

Thought for the day: God is present and at work, steadily and unceasingly.

Sarah Sanderson (Oregon, US)

PRAYER FOCUS: HEALTH WORKERS
* Words by Walter Chalmers Smith, 1867

WEDNESDAY 25 MAY

A Misguided GPS

Read James 1:2–8
There is a way that appears to be right, but in the end it leads to death.
Proverbs 14:12 (NIV)

The headline read, 'Man Follows Sat-Nav Directions and Drives Car into River'. The driver of the car said he was travelling at night, the road was dark and the weather was foggy. He believed that the directions his sat-nav gave him were correct, unaware that the unfamiliar road ahead ended in disaster.

As I read the newspaper article, I began to think how easily we can be misled or distracted as we travel through life. Our world can offer any number of tempting paths, which may or may not prove to be the right direction for us. Other people can persuade us to think that we are making right choices. But sometimes those options can lead us down roads that are potentially dangerous.

Fortunately, through prayer, we can ask God for daily guidance and wisdom to know which paths are right for us. From God we can receive the kind of wisdom that goes beyond human reasoning. Centring our lives in daily prayer helps us to find the way, guiding us toward joyful living and an eternal home.

Prayer: *Dear heavenly Father, thank you for guiding us through life. Thank you for your wisdom that shows us what to do when we are faced with difficult decisions. Amen*

Thought for the day: Before making decisions, I will pray and listen for God's answer.

Jerry Bragalone (Pennsylvania, US)

PRAYER FOCUS: SOMEONE FACING A DIFFICULT DECISION

THURSDAY 26 MAY

Why Pray?

Read 1 John 5:14–15
You do not have, because you do not ask.
James 4:2 (NRSV)

Prayer is one way we have of serving God. It is not our means of getting him to do our will on earth but a means of getting his will done on earth. As we pray, God helps us find solutions to the numerous puzzling and painful situations of our lives. His wisdom surely exceeds ours. When we do not know what the will of God is, prayer will help us discern it.

The verse quoted above reminds us that we must ask in order to receive. If the Syrophoenician woman had not challenged Jesus, her daughter would not have been cured (see Mark 7:24–30). If the blind man of Jericho had not called out to Jesus, he would have remained blind (see Luke 18:35–43).

Just as we do not know who will respond to the message of Jesus until we share it, we will never see the results of a prayer that was not prayed. We pray to acknowledge our faith in God and to find the power to be his people in the world.

Prayer: *Eternal God, teach us how to pray as we should and according to your will. May you be glorified in our lives, because we come always to you in prayer. Amen*

Thought for the day: 'The prayer of a righteous person is powerful and effective' (James 5:16, NIV).

Francisco de Castro Maria (Luanda, Angola)

PRAYER FOCUS: THOSE WHO HAVE DIFFICULTY PRAYING

FRIDAY 27 MAY

Finding Our Way

Read Numbers 14:1–11

'You have spoken arrogantly against me,' says the Lord, 'Yet you ask, "What have we said against you?"'
Malachi 3:13 (NIV)

As a volunteer tutor at a community centre, I had been assigned to help a student named Tony with his maths homework. For more than an hour I worked with him, but Tony was not interested in my tips. In fact, during most of the tutoring session, he grumbled and complained, explaining that he did not see any value in learning maths. After listening to his complaints, I began to tell him why I thought maths was important. Several minutes later, Tony looked at his maths problems, apologised for his behaviour and said that he was ready to work on his assignment.

It does not take much for us to start complaining. Just like the Israelites in today's reading from Numbers, we too can find ourselves grumbling and expressing our doubts toward God. Often these doubts come as a result of not understanding what he is doing in our lives. But God knows what is best for us and has a plan for us. If we obey him and rest securely in his promises, God will open our hearts and our minds, enabling us to see the way ahead.

Prayer: *Dear Lord, help us to remain faithful to you, as you have been to us. Amen*

Thought for the day: In times of doubt or frustration, I can draw near to God.

James C. Hendrix (Indiana, US)

PRAYER FOCUS: VOLUNTEER TUTORS

SATURDAY 28 MAY

Showers of Blessings

Read Matthew 25:31–40
What are human beings that you are mindful of them, mortals that you care for them?
Psalm 8:4 (NRSV)

Early one cold, winter morning, I stood outside watching the streaking meteors of the Leonid meteor shower. As I viewed the celestial performance, I thought about the constancy of God's love. I tried to imagine God's Spirit hovering over the surface of the Earth and developing our planet into a living ecosystem.

As I continued to feel the chill in spite of my warm clothing, my thoughts turned to those enduring cold without adequate clothing or even sufficient food. I wondered, 'If I were cold and hungry, would I be looking at the night sky and marvelling at the majesty of creation in the same way?'

Each star in the vast sky is only one, but together the stars form powerful, stunning galaxies. In today's reading Jesus reminds us that we are not alone in this world. He calls us to show compassion. Regardless of how seemingly minor, our kindnesses to one another have the same value as showing kindness to Jesus. Compassion for the needy is not to be taken lightly, even if we are tempted to think that small efforts cannot make a difference. With the psalmist, we marvel that amidst this vast universe, God cares for each of us. As he pours out grace on us, we can share this grace with others.

Prayer: *Majestic Lord and Creator, bless our efforts to serve you. Help us to care for the hurting people of our planet in the holy name of Jesus Christ. Amen*

Thought for the day: I honour the Lord when I give as I am able.

Gael Stuart Phaneuf (Colorado, US)

PRAYER FOCUS: THOSE LIVING IN POVERTY

SUNDAY 29 MAY

God's Steadfast Love

Read Romans 8:31–39

This is love: it is not that we loved God but that he loved us and sent his Son as the sacrifice that deals with our sins.
1 John 4:10 (CEB)

In my sixth year of church ministry, I went through a divorce. It was complicated, and I lived through several years of shame and despair. Yet during this painful experience, I came to know God's miraculous grace. His unconditional love was evident in the support of my family, my friends and the church I served. Thanks to their love and encouragement, I was able to continue with my pastoral responsibilities, caring for others even during the divorce process.

I am living proof of the healing God brings through grace. In my heart, I have only gratitude because my life is a gift from God. His unconditional love heals, restores and makes all things new.

This experience gave me a new perspective so that I could serve as an instrument of grace to others. I learned that God expects us to love others unconditionally, as he loves us. Nothing, neither our failures nor our flaws, can separate us from the love of God (see Romans 8:38–39).

Prayer: *Thank you, God, for your unconditional love. Help us to love others as you love us. Amen*

Thought for the day: God's grace can bring us all new life.

Eric A. Hernández Lopez (Puerto Rico)

PRAYER FOCUS: MINISTERS GOING THROUGH DIVORCE

MONDAY 30 MAY

More than an Option

Read Proverbs 3:1–8
In all your ways acknowledge him, and he will make straight your paths.
Proverbs 3:6 (NRSV)

I was walking my dog in our neighbourhood on a beautiful spring evening. Along the way, I observed a grandfather who was on an outing with his two small granddaughters. When they neared the road, the grandfather told his younger granddaughter, who had run ahead, 'Don't cross the street until I can get there to watch for cars!' The little girl proceeded to cross the street without looking right or left. No cars were coming, so she was safe; the grandfather smiled at me ruefully and said, 'I guess every direction I give her is an option.'

It occurred to me that we often treat God's word in the same way. Rather than listening to and living in his word, we charge ahead, confident that we can make it on our own. When we run into difficulties, we realise that we need scripture to help us cope with the dangers and pitfalls of life. Fortunately for us, God loves us, forgives our lapses and cares for us, even when we forget and treat his word as optional.

Prayer: *Dear Lord, remind us to study your word and to walk in your ways throughout our lives. Amen*

Thought for the day: God's word is a daily help to us.

Jayne E. Parker (Florida, US)

PRAYER FOCUS: GRANDPARENTS AND GRANDCHILDREN

TUESDAY 31 MAY

Still Serving

Read Isaiah 46:3–4

[The righteous] will bear fruit even when old and grey; they will remain lush and fresh in order to proclaim: 'The Lord is righteous. He's my rock. There's nothing unrighteous in him.'
Psalm 92:14–15 (CEB)

I met Ava in a sheltered housing complex. She embodied the vision of the psalmist who wrote that even in our old age, God will lead us to love. Ava had spent her working life as a seamstress. Even in her nineties, she could turn gifts of fabric into beautifully crafted blouses and skirts or trousers and shirts for the homeless.

When Ava's hands got too stiff and her eyes too dim, she became discouraged. Then one day she noticed that the small packets of biscuits beside each place in the dining room often went uneaten. When she began to collect the packets, her friends noticed and began saving them for her. When she had filled a bag, she would call a church member to take it to the local food bank.

One day a resident asked Ava with exasperation: 'Why do you care? You're old now. It's time to think about yourself!' Ava just smiled and kept on collecting biscuits and passing them on. Hers was a practical, hands-on faith.

Ava is gone now, but she remains an example of faithful living. I won't forget the lesson I learned from her—to look at what's in front of me and find a way to help someone in need.

Prayer: *Dear God, help us see your world and your people with eyes wide open. Grant us the courage to offer what we can when we see a need. Amen*

Thought for the day: Even in old age, God will lead us to serve others.

Carol J. Allen (Illinois, US)

PRAYER FOCUS: RESIDENTS OF RETIREMENT COMMUNITIES

WEDNESDAY 1 JUNE

More Than We Can Handle

Read 2 Corinthians 1:8–11
God rescued us from a terrible death, and he will rescue us. We have set our hope on him that he will rescue us again.
2 Corinthians 1:10 (CEB)

Statements from well-meaning friends such as, 'God will not give you more than you can handle', often cannot provide the comfort one hopes to receive when going through a difficult situation. Sometimes in these situations we feel as if we need to put on a façade of faith while we remain inwardly broken.

Paul had a different point of view on dealing with hardships. Pressed on every side, he confessed that his trials were, in fact, more than he could bear. But in the same breath he proclaimed God's faithfulness and his belief that God would deliver him. His hope was set on God's promises, but he also knew he needed the prayers of his community to support him.

Sometimes we bear burdens so heavy that we are left in a place of despair. But we still have hope because God is with the brokenhearted. When we are not suffering, we can take time to notice those around us who may be weary and wounded. We can lift them up in prayer and cry out to God on their behalf. When we pray for one another, we can set our hope on God that he will rescue us again.

Prayer: *Dear Lord, help us to know that even when we are incapable of handling life's struggles, you are completely sufficient to bear our burdens and strengthen us. Amen*

Thought for the day: I can place my hope in God.

Denise DuBois Pass (Virginia, US)

PRAYER FOCUS: SOMEONE EXPERIENCING ANXIETY

THURSDAY 2 JUNE

Heavenly Rewards

Read Matthew 5:3–12
Rejoice and be glad, for your reward is great in heaven.
Matthew 5:12 (NRSV)

Many organisations talk about the rewards of retirement. In Thailand, some organisations offer retirement pay, some honour the work you have done for the company in other ways. But the great reward of God is different.

Today's reading tells us how our rewards are great in heaven. We can learn a lot about how God wants us to live from this passage. Verse three reminds us to be conscious and humble that our lives are not perfect and that we need God's help and his grace. We learn that to be pure in heart is to be one with God and to live for him. Jesus ends by teaching us to be prepared to serve God by making peace in our communities and societies even when we face injustice, persecution or scandal.

God prepares a great reward in heaven for those who live their lives in this way. As our reading says, 'Rejoice and be glad, for your reward is great in heaven' (Matthew 5:12).

Prayer: *Loving God, help us believe and trust that you have prepared the way for our lives. In the name of Jesus Christ, we pray. Amen*

Thought for the day: My reward in heaven is greater than any reward on earth.

Prasartporn Tariyo (Chiang Mai, Thailand)

PRAYER FOCUS: PEOPLE APPROACHING RETIREMENT

FRIDAY 3 JUNE

Hidden Blessings

Read Romans 5:1–5
We know that all things work together for good to them that love God, to them who are the called according to his purpose.
Romans 8:28 (KJV)

After months of procrastination, I went to a dermatologist to have a suspicious mole on my arm examined. To my surprise, the doctor wanted to take a biopsy from another spot on my skin—one that hadn't concerned me at all. When the results came back, the second site, rather than the first, had been diagnosed as early-stage melanoma, a deadly form of skin cancer. Thankfully, the problem was discovered while it could be treated and before it had spread to other parts of my body.

I had prayed for the first mole to simply disappear without medical intervention; yet if God had answered my prayer, the serious health situation in the other spot would have gone undiscovered. The result could have been fatal.

So often we pray for the removal of circumstances that are difficult or challenging and we get frustrated when they persist. Instead, we can thank God for the good that he will bring out of difficult circumstances. The result may be more favourable than we can see or imagine. We are blessed by God's love and protection, even when we are unaware that a problem exists.

Prayer: *Dear God, we thank you for seeing beyond our prayers and using negative circumstances in our lives to bring about a greater good. Amen*

Thought for the day: God can bring blessings out of difficult circumstances.

Elaine L. Bridge (Ohio, US)

PRAYER FOCUS: DERMATOLOGISTS

SATURDAY 4 JUNE

Good Connections

Read Galatians 3:24–29

Jesus said, 'My prayer is not for [those you have given me] alone. I pray also for those who will believe in me through their message, that all of them may be one.'
John 17:20–21 (NIV)

Reading an *Upper Room* devotional written by a woman from Russia helped me think about the greatness and goodness of God. I wondered what kind of family she had. Did she work outside the home? What was her daily life like? Even though I didn't know her personally, I felt a bond of faith with her. I prayed for her and marvelled at the connection we have through our faith in the Lord, even though we live thousands of miles apart.

This bond of faith happens each day in my devotional time as I read *The Upper Room*. The writer may be from England or Ethiopia, Australia or the United States, or anywhere else in the world. The experiences they write about always help me in some way and strengthen my faith. I pray for those who share their faith in writing and for those who work to bring this magazine into publication.

We can also feel a strong bond with those closest to us—those in our neighbourhood, our church, our families and at work. Paul wrote, 'Clothe yourselves with love, which binds everything together in perfect harmony' (Colossians 3:14, NRSV). No matter where we live, God's love gives us the enduring joy of knowing that we are connected to God and to others by love and faith.

Prayer: *Thank you, God, for your gracious love for us that enables us to connect with one another. Amen*

Thought for the day: We are connected to one another through God's love.

Joan S. Hutcheson (Georgia, US)

PRAYER FOCUS: THE STAFF AND WRITERS OF *THE UPPER ROOM*

SUNDAY 5 JUNE

A Gentle Answer

Read Proverbs 15:1–4
A gentle answer turns away wrath.
Proverbs 15:1 (NIV)

Recently someone accused me of doing something I had not done. No matter how I defended myself, my words had no effect. He disregarded my position and said things that hurt my feelings. I remember my face growing hot and wanting to lash out at him with angry words. Then I realised that acknowledging my feelings and defending myself may have been fine, but reacting solely out of anger could harm him as much as his words had harmed me.

So instead of lashing out, I decided to spend time with God in quiet prayer and reflection. Talking over my hurt and anger with God helped to calm me down. I found that I needed to rely on God's power to give me strength to respond in loving ways. I remembered the verse quoted above, 'A gentle answer turns away wrath, but a harsh word stirs up anger.'

When our feelings have been hurt, we may want to speak back in anger. Instead, God encourages us to break the bitter cycle of anger with a gentle response.

Prayer: *Dear God, help us consider our words before we speak them, so that what comes out of our mouths will help, not hurt. Amen*

Thought for the day: With God's help I will use my words wisely.

Thomas E. Fuller (Oregon, US)

PRAYER FOCUS: SOMEONE WHO HAS HURT ME

MONDAY 6 JUNE

Love

Read 1 Corinthians 13:4–8

God is love, and those who abide in love abide in God, and God abides in them.
1 John 4:16 (NRSV)

At my nephew's wedding I was asked to read a paraphrase of today's reading from 1 Corinthians. Even though it was a civil ceremony and God wasn't mentioned, he was present, because love was there.

We as Christians are called to love our neighbour as ourselves (see Matthew 19:19). If we can celebrate human love—a love that is dim compared to God's love—how much more can we celebrate God's pure love for each and every person we meet?

My nephew's wedding was a reminder to me of how much God loves everyone. He is calling me to love not only my family but also those around me whom I don't always find lovable—those I sometimes disparage, those outside my comfort zone, those I find scary. God loves us all, and we are called to do the same.

Prayer: *Dear Father, help us to be reflections of that love. We pray the prayer Jesus taught us, saying, 'Our Father which art in heaven, Hallowed be thy name. Thy kingdom come. Thy will be done in earth, as it is in heaven. Give us this day our daily bread. And forgive us our debts, as we forgive our debtors. And lead us not into temptation, but deliver us from evil: For thine is the kingdom, and the power, and the glory, for ever.'* Amen*

Thought for the day: Who is God calling me to love today?

Carol Denereaz (New South Wales, Australia)

PRAYER FOCUS: MY NON-CHRISTIAN FAMILY AND FRIENDS
* Matthew 6:9–13 (KJV)

TUESDAY 7 JUNE

Unclean Rags

Read Ephesians 2:4–14
All our righteous acts are like filthy rags.
Isaiah 64:6 (NIV)

Growing up on a farm, we were always doing dirty jobs, such as shovelling manure. We learned to repair everything we could ourselves to save money. Once we worked for days trying to replace a clutch on an old tractor. By the time it was done, I was covered with grease, oil and dirt.

That day my life was just as dirty on the inside because of my sin. In my mind I felt I was all right because I was doing all the religious things I was supposed to do. Then I read the Bible verse that said 'all our righteous acts are like filthy rags'. At that moment, I knew I could never be good enough to merit God's love.

One of the greatest acts of love that God shows us is grace—his forgiveness when we don't deserve it. Grace is a gift, impossible to earn. Living a good life is important, but we will never be clean enough just by doing good things. We can enjoy God's grace because Jesus died on the cross for our sins and was raised to new life. When we commit our lives to Christ and rely on God's grace, we can experience new life as well.

Prayer: *Loving God, thank you for sending your Son to die on the cross for us so that our sins may be forgiven. Amen*

Thought for the day: I am made clean by Christ.

Kenn Edwards (New Mexico, US)

PRAYER FOCUS: MECHANICS

WEDNESDAY 8 JUNE

Angels in Disguise

Read Hebrews 13:1–3

A good tree cannot bear bad fruit, and a bad tree cannot bear good fruit… Thus, by their fruit you will recognise them.
Matthew 7: 18, 20 (NIV)

Frank lives in a tent by the airport. He is 67, homeless and mostly keeps to himself. People avoid Frank because of his situation and rough image. Those who do, misjudge him; I know I did. As I've got to know Frank, I've learned that he has a kind and generous heart. He cares for a homeless woman and her cat that live nearby. He feeds the birds and squirrels who live around him. Frank just might be an angel in disguise (see Hebrews 13:2).

It's easy to leap to conclusions and to misjudge others. We tend to notice the outward things: their clothes, where they live, how they talk. But Jesus told us we can recognise the character of another person by their 'fruit'.

Fruit takes time to develop and grow. Over time we will get to know others by the 'fruit' that the Holy Spirit grows not only in them but in us as well. The apostle Paul lists that fruit: 'love, joy, peace, patience, kindness, goodness, gentleness, and self-control' (Galatians 5:22–24, CEB).

When we take the time to get to know the people around us, we allow ourselves to see the real fruit they possess. We may discover angels in disguise around us.

Prayer: *Thank you, God, for the people around us who bless us and make life worth living. Amen*

Thought for the day: Which of the Spirit's fruit do I need to cultivate?

Chad McComas (Oregon, US)

THURSDAY 9 JUNE

God's Surprises

Read 1 Kings 19:1–13

What no eye has seen, what no ear has heard, and what no human mind has conceived—the things God has prepared for those who love him.
1 Corinthians 2:9 (NIV)

We read in the story from 1 Kings 19 that even the great prophet Elijah experienced fear and discouragement. God dealt with him kindly and gently, surprising him with an angel and a still small voice.

At times in my life, I have been surprised by the warmth and peace of God's Holy Spirit, filling me and reassuring me that God is with me and that he is all I need. When I am surprised by the laughter of kookaburras visiting my garden, I remember that 'the joy of the Lord is your strength' (Nehemiah 8:10). The beauty of the stars in the sky on a clear, dark night surprises me with the knowledge of God's creativity and magnitude. The unexpected gift of a meal from my church family surprises me with the reminder that God knows my every need. The ways God cares for me never cease to surprise and encourage me. I want to share this joy and encouragement with others.

The surprises of our loving Creator never end. How amazing to realize that God prepares for us surprises that are what we need when we need them.

Prayer: *Thank you, God, for tenderly caring for us. Open our hearts to the surprises with which you bless us. Amen*

Thought for the day: God's surprises never end.

Ann Stewart (South Australia, Australia)

PRAYER FOCUS: SOMEONE WHO IS DISCOURAGED

FRIDAY 10 JUNE

A Good Foundation

Read 1 Corinthians 3:5–11
No one can lay any foundation other than the one that has been laid; that foundation is Jesus Christ.
1 Corinthians 3:11 (NRSV)

I grew up in a small rural village in Gujarat, India. When I was old enough, my parents sent me to a Christian boarding school. Though I received a good education, the school was not funded properly, and we never had enough to eat. I cannot think of a day during my four years at the school when I did not go to bed hungry.

But when I look back I have very fond memories of the school. During my years at the school, I came to know the Lord and my education built a good foundation for the rest of my life.

Because I am so grateful for the seeds of faith that the school gave me, I have made a commitment to visit the school every year to help the children and to meet some of their needs. I provide a good meal and a small, practical gift for each child. After the meal, the children greet me and receive their gifts. Each child hugs me and says, 'Thank you, Uncle. God bless you.' Being able to help the children of the school where the seeds of faith were first planted in me is one of the greatest joys and blessings of my life.

In our reading, Paul reminds the Corinthians that seeds of faith can be planted in many ways, but it is 'God who gives the growth' (v. 6). When we show compassion and nurture the faith of others, we help to lay the foundation of Christ for future generations.

Prayer: *God, our Father, be gracious to us and give us generous hearts that we may share with those in need. Amen*

Thought for the day: How can I share my blessings with someone who needs them today?

Ishwarbhai Hirabhai Dabhi (Gujarat, India)

PRAYER FOCUS: CHILDREN IN BOARDING SCHOOLS

SATURDAY 11 JUNE

Enough

Read Judges 7:15–25

God will meet all your needs according to the riches of his glory in Christ Jesus.
Philippians 4:19 (NIV)

Recently my husband saw a need for young families in our community to have a time of meeting together and encouragement. He suggested we host a monthly gathering in our home, and I laughed. All I could see was that we didn't have enough space, time, energy or money.

When I overcame my fear of not having enough and allowed God to use us, he did great things. People made new friends, old friends reconnected, we encouraged one another in faith and we supported one another through life's challenges.

I can relate to Gideon's doubts that God could use him when he asked, 'How can I save Israel? My clan is the weakest in Manasseh, and I am the least in my family' (Judges 6:15). God showed Gideon that no matter how little he had, with God's help, he would have enough.

When God asks us to do something and we feel we don't have enough, we can remember that God supplies the strength and everything we need to do his work.

Prayer: *Dear Lord, help us to step out in faith and to serve you whenever you ask. Amen*

Thought for the day: No matter how little I have, with God's help, I have enough.

Amelia Rhodes (Michigan, US)

PRAYER FOCUS: MY COMMUNITY OF FRIENDS AND NEIGHBOURS

SUNDAY 12 JUNE

The Greatest of These

Read Acts 1:6–11

You will receive power when the Holy Spirit has come upon you; and you will be my witnesses… to the ends of the earth.
Acts 1:8 (NRSV)

When I befriended a 95-year-old woman in our community, I hoped to add joy to her days. I had much to learn. In my frequent visits with her during the three years before her death, I learned that I had overestimated what I could bring to her and underestimated what she had to offer me. Early on, I felt a deep connection between us, even though we were different in age, race, economic status and educational background. The greatest lesson I learned was that none of our differences prevented meaningful friendship.

Each time she welcomed me into her home, she manoeuvred her power-operated wheelchair close enough to hold my hands. I loved spending time with her and learning from her deep spiritual insight.

'The Lord has brought us together,' she said. 'The Holy Spirit has come upon us.'

Now, as I drive by her empty house, I hear her voice saying again, 'We must read the word, and we must live the word.' I know that she has gone on to be with Christ. I can best honour our friendship by sharing the gifts she so graciously bestowed on me.

Prayer: *Thank you, God, for people who bring us closer to you. Give us the desire to be faithful to your word. Amen*

Thought for the day: Today I will love others as God loves me.

Dianne T. Evans (South Carolina, US)

PRAYER FOCUS: TO SEEK WISDOM FROM SOMEONE DIFFERENT FROM ME

MONDAY 13 JUNE

Finding Rest

Read Psalm 62:1–8
Jesus said, 'Come with me by yourselves to a quiet place and get some rest.'
Mark 6:31 (NIV)

Often I would find myself overstressed and running on fumes—and ending up exhausted and grumpy. My to-do-list would grow longer every day, and I longed to escape to some desert island. Then, one exhausting day, I heard God speaking to my churning mind with the words from Psalm 62: 'My soul finds rest in God alone' (v. 1). How I longed for this rest! And I knew that this kind of soul-satisfying rest comes only from God.

As a way of seeking this rest, I began taking 15 to 20 minutes during a busy day to slow down and be alone with God. The time and the location varied. Sometimes, I went for a walk or found a quiet place to sit. I would talk with God about the pressures of that day. One afternoon, I wondered why God allows human beings to get tired. I thought that he could have created us so that we are perpetually energised, never exhausted. And then I realised that tiredness may be Jesus' calling us to himself. At these times, like a worn-out child, I need to snuggle into the lap of Jesus and hear him say, 'Come to me, all you who are weary and burdened, and I will give you rest' (Matthew 11:28).

Prayer: *Creator God, thank you for giving us rest in you. We come, weary and tired, to find strength in your presence. Renew us and sustain us with your love. Amen*

Thought for the day: Taking time to rest with God each day can renew and refresh me.

Dave Beckwith (California, US)

PRAYER FOCUS: SOMEONE OVERWHELMED BY STRESS

TUESDAY 14 JUNE

God, the Great Cheese Maker

Read 1 Corinthians 3:1–9

I planted the seed, Apollos watered it, but God has been making it grow.
1 Corinthians 3:6 (NIV)

I am often stressed out by the enormity of the world's problems—hunger, war, human rights abuse—and my inability to do anything to help. I do try. I volunteer for a few hours, and I give some money to charity, but my efforts feel so small. I wish I could do more. I wish I could solve the world's problems.

I recently saw a story on TV about a man who raises sheep and makes cheese from their milk. It is painstaking work and needs a strong arm and lots of patience. The story got me thinking. For making cheese, the sheep produce the raw ingredient: milk. The cheese maker is the one who transforms the milk, creating a wonderful final product. Keeping the creamery running takes the milk of a lot of sheep, and each sheep is valued.

Believers are like those sheep. We can live faithful lives in our pasture and focus on making a simple raw ingredient: showing God's love to the people around us. God is the master cheese maker who transforms our efforts into real change for the world.

Prayer: *Dear Lord, help us to see that even though our efforts seem inconsequential, they are the raw materials you use to build up your kingdom. Amen*

Thought for the day: I can trust God to transform my small efforts for the good of the world.

Jennifer Oxley (Washington, US)

WEDNESDAY 15 JUNE

Clothed in Love

Read Colossians 3:12–17
One who forgives an affront fosters friendship, but one who dwells on disputes will alienate a friend.
Proverbs 17:9 (NRSV)

My friend Marie had worked for a company for many years. She was efficient and well liked, and her work was impeccable. However, her position was given to the niece of a new board member, and Marie had no choice but to pack up and leave. Before she left, however, Marie cleaned up her computer files and made them accessible to the new employee. She dusted and cleaned her bookshelves, and left leaving pens and newly sharpened pencils in a colourful desk-tidy. She made a short guidebook of helpful hints for the new worker and on her last day she thanked the people who had given her the job initially.

'But why would you do that for them when they let you go for no reason?' I questioned. 'I am going to leave as a Christian,' she said. 'I want my name to be associated with kindness and to show the love I always felt at doing my job.'

In his letter to the Colossians, Paul speaks of the 'clothes' that followers of Christ are to wear: compassion, kindness, humility, forgiveness and love, with love being 'above all'. Marie left her place of employment with kindness. She was wearing all the right 'clothes' and showed us the power of forgiveness and of Christ's love.

Prayer: *Creator God, even in adverse circumstances, help us to share your love and grace with everyone around us. Amen*

Thought for the day: When I replace anger with forgiveness, God gives me peace.

Jean L. Croyle (Pennsylvania, US)

PRAYER FOCUS: SOMEONE WHO HAS RECENTLY LOST A JOB

THURSDAY 16 JUNE

Unending Love

Read John 13:1–17

When Jesus knew that his hour was come that he should depart out of this world unto the Father, having loved his own which were in the world, he loved them unto the end.

John 13:1 (KJV)

My friend and I had once been ministers in the same town. Some years later I learned that he had been diagnosed with an inoperable brain tumour. He lay in a hospital bed awaiting radiation treatment. But his spirits were high. While he was unable to perform his duties, church members had stepped in and demonstrated their love. Members of his church had visited him while others had preached in his place.

When the news is bad or when tragedy strikes, I am tempted to think God has forgotten me. I've heard many propose that it's wrong to question God, but I believe that asking him a question can be helpful. Inquiring of God why something has happened and how I should respond to it is an expression of faith in his unending love.

Regardless of what touches our lives, God has not stopped loving us. He has loved us in the past, loves us in the present and will love us eternally. Even when we have questions, we can learn to trust his love, mercy and goodness.

Prayer: *Thank you, God, for eternal love that holds us throughout our lives. Amen*

Thought for the day: God welcomes my questions.

Martin Wiles (South Carolina, US)

PRAYER FOCUS: CONGREGATIONS WITHOUT MINISTERS

FRIDAY 17 JUNE

Lessons from a Violet

Read James 5:13–18
The prayer of a righteous person is powerful and effective.
James 5:16 (NIV)

After returning from a long holiday, I retrieved my African violets from a friend. Three of the four plants had lovely purple flowers and deep green leaves. The fourth had soft, yellow leaves and no blooms. I was surprised, but then I recalled that I hadn't seen blossoms on that plant for at least two years.

Patiently, I continued to water all my violets, even the fourth plant. Gradually, its leaves turned from pure yellow to a pretty shade of yellow-green, but it remained flowerless. Eventually a tiny purple flower appeared! It seemed to be hiding under the leaves—just waiting to be discovered. Then, more blooms popped up among the now-green leaves. Each day brought me joy as I checked for more flowers.

What spiritual life lessons this hardy little plant provided! God is with us, even when we least expect it. Patience, persistence, faith and prayer will bring us blessings. How many of us have found our prayers answered after we have already given up hope! We may encounter people and situations that turn out to be just the answer to our prayers. Like the unexpected bloom, situations like these remind us that God is working in our lives.

Prayer: *Dear God, help us to be hopeful and to trust you. May we always expect your nearness, protection, guidance and love. Amen*

Thought for the day: God's answers to prayer can transcend anything I can imagine.

Linda Kinde (Florida, US)

PRAYER FOCUS: SOMEONE IN NEED OF HOPE

SATURDAY 18 JUNE

New Clothes!

Read Ephesians 4:20–24

You have taken off your old self with its practices and have put on the new self.
Colossians 3:9–10 (NIV)

When the weather starts to get warmer I think about clothes. Summer clothes! Out comes the big suitcase from under the bed, and soon I'm unpacking last summer's wardrobe and planning new additions for the coming season. Exciting! Especially when I realise I'll soon be setting my mostly dark-coloured winter clothes aside for all those colourful summer ones. A joy indeed!

This has brought to life for me some Bible words about clothes which show that turning our lives around to live in God's way is like putting off one set of undesirable clothes in order to wear a whole new attractive outfit—God's good and wise purpose for us. What a joy to set aside our old way of life and embrace a new and fulfilling life with God.

Prayer: *Lord, help me to set aside my 'old clothes' and instead put on a whole 'new outfit'. Amen*

Thought for the day: In Christ I have a whole new self.

Elaine Brown (Perthshire, Scotland)

PRAYER FOCUS: NEW CHRISTIANS

SUNDAY 19 JUNE

Running with God

Read Matthew 6:5–15
When you pray, go into your room, close the door and pray to your Father, who is unseen. Then your Father, who sees what is done in secret, will reward you.
Matthew 6:6 (NIV)

I am a runner and over the past 40 years, I have stepped out of my house and greeted the day with the step-by-step rhythm of my feet. Some people have asked me if I run with headphones, listening to music. I do not. I find that I am better able to have my daily conversations with God if I have no other sounds to distract me.

These morning runs have become my prayer room, and I am thankful for this quiet time with God. This setting is a holy place for me.

My chats with God range from praying for family members or the needs of friends to asking him for guidance and direction for my life. God is always listening as the dawn is breaking around me. Sometimes answers and results come quickly; others I still wait for, knowing that I may never see a resolution in my lifetime.

Through my own prayer practice, I have come to understand that our prayer practices are as unique as God has made each of us.

Prayer: *Dear Lord, we are thankful that you allow us to pray at any time and in any place. May we be faithful in keeping our appointments with you. As Jesus taught us, we pray, 'Father, hallowed be your name, your kingdom come. Give us each day our daily bread. Forgive us our sins, for we also forgive everyone who sins against us. And lead us not into temptation.'* Amen*

Thought for the day: Where is my prayer room?

Colleen Forshee (Pennsylvania, US)

PRAYER FOCUS: RUNNERS
* Luke 11:2–4 (NIV)

MONDAY 20 JUNE

Who Am I to Complain?

Read Psalm 8:1–9

Will we receive good from God but not also receive bad?
Job 2:10 (CEB)

One morning I listened to the radio as a minister shared her life story. She has many physical limitations, but has achieved much and remains joyful and grateful to the Lord. The fact that she dedicated her life to a ministry of service given all the suffering she endured impressed me.

It seems that many of us find it difficult to fulfil the potential for which we were created or to establish a devotional life even when we are healthy and whole. I felt embarrassed that I had been griping about everyday irritations. I complain when it rains or does not rain enough, when it is cold or not cold enough. Sometimes it seems as if I can never be satisfied. So I was faced with the question: 'Who am I to complain?'

For many of us, complaining is such a regular habit that we hardly notice when we do it. It is more important to value what we have. Our hope lies in the gifts, talents and strengths we possess that can be used in God's service. We can recognise these blessings when we remember that God is always present with us.

Prayer: *Loving God, help us to stop complaining and to acknowledge all the blessings you have given us. Amen*

Thought for the day: I can serve the Lord with gladness.

Narda Luz Vargas (Dominican Republic)

PRAYER FOCUS: SOMEONE WITH PHYSICAL CHALLENGES

TUESDAY 21 JUNE

The Heart of the Matter

Read Matthew 22:34–40

Jesus said to [the lawyer], 'You shall love the Lord your God with all your heart, and with all your soul, and with all your mind.'
Matthew 22:37 (NRSV)

Several years ago at Christmas time, I went with my son and his family to see the 'Festival of Lights', a beautiful display of Christmas decorations and lights. As my grandchildren were taking in all the sights, my grandson, who was about six at the time, came up with a question: 'I wonder what Jesus wants for a birthday present?'

His twin sister quickly responded, 'Jack, Jesus doesn't want a present. He wants our love.'

My jaw dropped in amazement at this statement. I thought of all the scholarly books of theology I had read; nothing came close to the profound insight of this child's simple statement.

It's important that as Christians we know the doctrines essential to the history of our faith and that we are able to answer those who question the reason for our beliefs. But when it comes to devotion to our Lord Jesus, my granddaughter was right. Jesus is not interested in our works, our knowledge, our rituals or our presents. He just wants our love.

Prayer: *God of love, thank you for the gift of your Son. Help us to show our love for you and for him in the way we live our lives today. Amen*

Thought for the day: Love is the greatest gift we can offer to Jesus—or anyone.

Dewitt Watson (Ohio, US)

PRAYER FOCUS: CHILDREN LEARNING ABOUT FAITH

WEDNESDAY 22 JUNE

Nurturing

Read 1 John 4:7–12

If I speak in the tongues of men or of angels, but do not have love, I am only a resounding gong or a clanging cymbal.
1 Corinthians 13:1 (NIV)

As I looked down with satisfaction at my newly planted seedlings, I thought about how new believers need to be nurtured in a similar way to these young plants. Other Christians can do this by accepting new believers where they are on their Christian journeys, encouraging them through Bible study and supporting them with loving actions.

However, it is important to remember that our Christian formation is a life-long journey so that we do not become impatient with each other. Each person has his or her own lessons to learn. With God's help, we can develop a strong and deep root system and sturdy stems and branches to support the good fruit of faith. As we become firmly grounded in God's word, we gain a deeper knowledge and experience of his steadfast love. We can trust God whatever our circumstances are.

Just as I care for and nurture my plants, we can be sensitive to the faith journeys of others, providing encouragement and support. We can do this by being attentive to God, who helps us grow, and by always acting in love.

Prayer: *Dear Lord, thank you for placing loving people in our lives to help us grow in faith. Amen*

Thought for the day: Whom can I encourage on the journey of faith today?

Elaine Chipps (Western Province, South Africa)

PRAYER FOCUS: MY SPIRITUAL MENTORS

THURSDAY 23 JUNE

Fearful?

Read Philippians 4:6–8, 12–13
Do not fear, for I am with you; do not be dismayed, for I am your God. I will strengthen you and help you; I will uphold you with my righteous right hand.
Isaiah 41:10 (NIV)

When I was seven, I was afraid of the dark. If I had to get up at night, I would hold my pillow over my eyes and feel my way down the hall. One night I miscalculated and tumbled down the basement stairs. After that, I no longer put the pillow over my eyes.

As an adult, I face different fears: losing a loved one or someone breaking into my home at night. Yet in the Bible, God says, 'Do not fear, for I am with you.' This assurance leaves me with a choice. I can put the pillow over my eyes and fail to experience the courage and peace God offers. Or I can face my fears and trust him to help me. I've found that repeating uplifting Bible verses helps me to trust God and overcome my fear—verses like, 'I can do all things through him who strengthens me' (Philippians 4:13, NRSV) or 'I will lie down and sleep, for you alone, Lord, make me dwell in safety' (Psalm 4:8, NIV).

As we trust and obey God, our fears can fade away and we can open our eyes to his sustaining care for us.

Prayer: *Dear Father, when we're afraid, help us turn to you in faith and trust. Amen*

Thought for the day: I can trust God to be with me.

Carole Harmon (Idaho, US)

PRAYER FOCUS: CHILDREN IN FRIGHTENING SITUATIONS

FRIDAY 24 JUNE

The Path Before Us

Read Jeremiah 29:10–12

This is what the Lord says: 'Stand at the crossroads and look; ask for the ancient paths, ask where the good way is, and walk in it, and you will find rest for your souls.'
Jeremiah 6:16 (NIV)

A section of the Carolina Thread Trail winds through rural North Carolina. As I walked there one spring morning I listened for God and saw his creation. Birds sang, squirrels scurried up the trees, and deer dashed from my sight. The path bloomed with flowers of all colours. Ferns were slowly opening their tender fronds, and the water in the shallow stream gracefully flowed over the rocks.

Alone on the path I took time to think of my 30 years as a firefighter. Newly-retired, I was searching for direction. I prayed, 'God, where do you want me? What is my new purpose? How do I serve you now? What path do I take?' The sights and sounds of the wilderness provided these words that I believe were inspired by God: 'Walk the path I have laid before you.'

In the Bible, God has provided markers to give us direction in life. Other guidance may come in the form of an encouraging word from a friend, a note from a colleague or a church member. God places us where we need to be. We can be assured that he has a plan for us and will accompany us along the path.

Prayer: *Thank you, Father, for walking with us as we journey through this life. Amen*

Thought for the day: God provides the direction I need.

David L. Bullins (North Carolina, US)

PRAYER FOCUS: SOMEONE FACING RETIREMENT

SATURDAY 25 JUNE

Friendship

Read Job 2:11–13

Those who withhold kindness from a friend forsake the fear of the Almighty.
Job 6:14 (NRSV)

When Job was suffering, three friends came to comfort him. It took effort for them to be there with him. For seven days they simply supported him with the power of their presence. The fact that they went to him in his time of need demonstrates the compassion of true friendship. But if we keep reading, we discover that these friends eventually became tormentors. When Job broke his silence, his friends began to speak harshly to him. That was when their friendship turned into a burden for Job.

We can learn much, both positive and negative, from Job's friends about comforting those who are afflicted. Job's friends were alarmed by his situation. Perhaps it was their own discomfort that caused them to minimise and attempt to explain away Job's pain. God calls us to be good friends to those who are hurting. When someone is suffering, we can listen and trust that our silent presence may be enough.

Prayer: *Thank you, Lord, for your friendship. Help me to be a friend to those who are suffering. Amen*

Thought for the day: How can I be present with someone who is suffering?

Geraldine Nicholas (Alberta, Canada)

PRAYER FOCUS: SOMEONE WHO NEEDS A GOOD FRIEND

SUNDAY 26 JUNE

Burden

Read Matthew 11:28–30
Jesus said, 'My yoke is easy and my burden is light.'
Matthew 11:30 (NIV)

From the age of five I have carried the secret shame of abuse. I have been lonely and often have felt like damaged goods. At times this burden has seemed greater than I could bear. I have even had thoughts of suicide.

Though I had heard Matthew 11:28–30 many times, I never understood how Jesus' yoke was easy and his burden was light. But after many sessions of therapy, God showed me that I did not have to bear the shame and guilt of abuse because I was never at fault—and that my resting place is in Jesus and his love. God had not left me but had carried me for more than 30 years.

Forgiveness has been a large part of my journey. It was never about saying what happened was OK. It was about letting go of anger and bitterness as I let the love of Jesus into my heart. Now for me, the yoke and burden of Jesus is his love and sharing his hope with others. No matter what our circumstances are, Jesus takes our heavy burdens and offers us the yoke of his love.

Prayer: *Dear Lord, help us to learn to not allow our past to define who we are. Thank you, Jesus, for carrying our burden. Amen*

Thought for the day: Abuse does not define who I am in Jesus.

Michelle Nash (Mississippi, US)

PRAYER FOCUS: THOSE SUFFERING ABUSE

MONDAY 27 JUNE

Unimaginable Help

Read Exodus 3:7–8
Happy are those whose help is the God of Jacob, whose hope is in the Lord their God.
Psalm 146:5 (NRSV)

For four hundred years the Israelites were slaves in Egypt. From a human standpoint, their situation seemed hopeless. But God sent Moses to proclaim God's power and concern for the people. A seemingly hopeless situation was transformed by the unimaginable acts of God.

When Jesus was executed, his followers scattered, fearing that they would suffer the same fate. The ray of hope that Jesus' disciples had found in him died on that cross at Calvary. But the unimaginable power of God once again transformed a situation of despair. Christ's resurrection kindled a flame of hope that would never be extinguished.

Sometimes situations in our own lives and the news from around the world can cause us to despair. But the unimaginable acts of God still break through seemingly hopeless situations. Through faith and prayer, we can call on our loving God to enter in and give us hope once more.

Prayer: *Dear God, you have no limitations. When our imaginations and efforts reach their limits, give us courage to step out into the unknown—trusting in you to help us. Amen*

Thought for the day: When we can't see a way out, God offers help in unimaginable ways.

Richard Woodard (Washington DC, US)

PRAYER FOCUS: SOMEONE FACING A SEEMINGLY HOPELESS SITUATION

TUESDAY 28 JUNE

Foolish Moxie

Read Luke 12:22–31

Humble yourselves under God's power so that he may raise you up in the last day. Throw all your anxiety onto him, because he cares about you.
1 Peter 5:6-7 (CEB)

Every week I go for a walk with a friend and Moxie, her medium-sized dog. Recently we saw a pair of big, black dogs approaching, and foolishly Moxie decided to take them on. My friend and the other dog owners managed to keep them apart, but I kept thinking that those dogs could have eaten Moxie for breakfast and looked around for more. A smart dog her size would have quietly put her owner between herself and the threat and hoped for the best.

During our walk, I had told my friend about a serious health challenge my husband is facing and how stressed I was with trying to work out all the details of finances, hospital visits and travel involved in his treatment. My wonderful friend began praying for me right then and there. Her promptness in bringing these needs before God reminded me that I have been spending more time fretting than asking God for what we need.

I realised later that Moxie and I have more in common than I'd like to admit. When stressful circumstances approach, I am too prone to rush at them, barking and snarling, heedless of how inadequate my own strength is. What I should be doing is putting the One who can handle anything in between me and my problems through prayer.

Prayer: *Thank you, God, for the prayers of family and friends. Help me to choose daily to pray instead of worrying. Amen*

Thought for the day: My worrying is useless; prayer is powerful.

Jennifer Aaron (Washington, US)

PRAYER FOCUS: FAMILIES DEALING WITH SERIOUS ILLNESS

WEDNESDAY 29 JUNE

'That's Fishing!'

Read Luke 5:1–11

Simon replied, 'Master, we've worked hard all night and caught nothing. But because you say so, I'll drop the nets.'
Luke 5:5 (CEB)

One of my friends invited me to go deep-sea fishing with him. I jumped at the opportunity for a new experience. It was a beautiful day with calm seas and a clear sky—but no fish! I asked my friend whether it was common not to catch anything. 'Oh, yes,' he said. 'That's fishing.' Some days, even an experienced angler who is doing everything right may not catch any fish. Fishing requires persistence, a focus on good practices and a willingness to accept any result.

Our spiritual practices of prayer, worship, holy conversation and working for justice, to name just a few, can often seem like that fishing trip. Even when we 'do everything right', it sometimes feels as if it all has no effect. Like learning to fish, learning how to be a disciple requires persistence, good practice and a sense of peace—whatever the outcome. We keep trying, with the faith that even when 'we've worked hard all night and caught nothing', Jesus is present with us, giving us a sense of purpose in his service.

Prayer: *Dear God, give us the patience to persist in discipleship even when we feel as if we are achieving little. Help us to be faithful, even as you are faithful. In the name of Jesus, we pray. Amen*

Thought for the day: Whatever happens, I can have faith that Jesus can work in me and through me.

David Hosey (North Carolina, US)

PRAYER FOCUS: THOSE FEELING SPIRITUALLY EMPTY

THURSDAY 30 JUNE

Dark Clouds of Blessing

Read 2 Corinthians 4:16–18
[Lord,] darkness and light are the same to you.
Psalm 139:12 (GNB)

It had been one of those mixed days in the hospital. I had shared one family's fearful thoughts of imminent death and bereavement. Then came a radiant young person's greeting: 'Good news! The tests are clear. I'm going home tomorrow!'

I sat for a moment in the car park looking out on the dark wooded hills below a summer sky. To my left hung clouds like curtains around a window of blue: on one side fluffy white, like cotton-wool balls, and on the other dark, brooding and storm-threatening pillars. It came to me that both cloud curtains contained the same droplets of water—blessings for the earth. The dark clouds just had greater blessings!

The joy and sadness mixed up in daily life may equally contain blessings. Living in Christ means that all our life events hold his love-gifts; the darker, more difficult days may well bring richer experiences of his grace. Holding on to his promise of 'always with you' may not take away the pain or answer the mystery questions, but we may learn the greater riches of trust and prayer, and be assured that the darkest cloud can hold the greatest blessing.

Prayer: *Lord, if this day brings hurt, give me the assurance that it is your day— a day of blessings. Amen*

Thought for the day: To the eye of faith dark skies are beautiful too.

Colin Harbach (Cumbria, UK)

PRAYER FOCUS: HOSPITAL PATIENTS

Prayer Workshop

Who Do You Say That I Am?

I started working as the editorial assistant for *The Upper Room* daily devotional guide at the beginning of 2015. I remember looking through the guide for the first time and thinking, 'This looks simple enough.' However, I continue to be surprised and fascinated by the complexity of this pocket-sized magazine and the wide array of cultures, ages and faith traditions that it represents.

As the editorial assistant, I spend a lot of time looking at the current and upcoming issues of the magazine, as well as past issues—sometimes from many years ago. I am always struck by the similarity of the prayers from long ago to the ones we pray today. I'm not sure why this surprises me. Maybe I expect that if Christians have been praying about the same issues for this long, surely we would have some answers by now. But what I find are people asking the same questions first posed thousands of years ago by Jesus' followers—questions such as: 'Who is my neighbour?' (Luke 10:29); 'What does this parable mean?' (see Luke 8:9); and 'How can this be?' (John 3:9, NIV). For decades the writers and readers of *The Upper Room* have prayerfully grappled with questions like these.

The Bible is candid about the difficulty of reconciling the mystery of God with our limited human understanding and the influence of this tension on our prayer lives. The psalmist cries out to God, while the writer of Ecclesiastes laments, 'Meaningless, meaningless, everything is meaningless!' (Ecclesiastes 1:2). Knowing that some of the most prominent figures in the Bible expressed their struggles in prayer comforts me and it reminds me that God does not require a single way to pray. Even when the apostles questioned Jesus on the correct formula for prayer, he offered an unexpectedly simple example: 'Your will be done... give us today our daily bread... forgive us our debts as we also have forgiven our debtors' (Matthew 6:9–13, NIV).

Prayer is a tradition shared by millions of people around the world. Part of the beauty of prayer is how unique the experience is for each person. I am touched when I read about the struggles and triumphs of the readers and writers of *The Upper Room*. Behind each meditation is a person who is like me in some ways but completely different in others. We may find common ground in the beliefs we hold and the questions we ask, but we are different in the kind of action our beliefs call us to, how we pray about our questions or what spiritual gifts we discover in ourselves. When I think about the worldwide community of Christ's followers I realise that while we all believe in Jesus, we choose experiences and words to express this belief that are just as unique as we are. Our answers to one of Jesus' great questions, 'Who do you say that I am?' (Matthew 16:15), are alike yet different. What a profound mystery! And what a great delight to be part of this community living out our faith through prayer together!

Questions for Reflection:

1. What examples of prayer do you find in the Bible? Which ones speak to you the most? Why? Are these examples similar to or different from the way you pray?

2. What does the inclusion of so many prayers of lament and frustration in the Bible tell us about how we should pray? What does Christ's model of prayer suggest about the nature of communicating with God?

3. What are some prayer practices that you haven't tried before (centring prayer, lectio divina, praying while engaged in a task, praying in nature)? How could one of these help you deepen your spiritual life?

Neely Baugh
Editorial Assistant

FRIDAY 1 JULY

The Pink Dolphin

Read Isaiah 43:1–7

Do not fear, for I have redeemed you; I have called you by name, you are mine.
Isaiah 43:1 (NRSV

I was fishing with a group of friends in south Louisiana when a pod of porpoises appeared. These social animals entertained us with synchronised leaps as pairs of them surfaced and playfully returned to the depths. We could hear them splashing and clearing their blow-holes as they circled the boat. They all looked the same to us—grey on top with white undersides.

Later, as we headed back up the channel, we saw a rare albino dolphin cavorting in front of a big commercial boat. It was pink!

It surged ahead of the boat, breaking the water, disappearing for a few seconds, and then gliding up out of the water again. As I watched, I realised that I was more excited to see this solitary dolphin than I had been to see the entire pod of porpoises. The experience reminded me that God sees the uniqueness of all creatures and finds great joy in them, even when they may not be readily understood and accepted by others.

We are all special creations of God whose love for each of us is unconditional. As Christians, we are called to show that same love and acceptance to others, even to those who may be very different from us.

Prayer: *Dear Lord, thank you for your unconditional love. Help us to celebrate the uniqueness of others just as you do. Amen*

Thought for the day: Each of us is unique in God's eyes.

David McCain (Louisiana, US)

PRAYER FOCUS: CONSERVATIONISTS

SATURDAY 2 JULY

The Power of God's Word

Read Psalm 19:7–11
The decrees of the Lord are firm, and all of them are righteous. They are more precious than gold, than much pure gold.
Psalm 19:9–10 (NIV)

Having worked for almost 20 years in the production and particularly in the proofreading of Christian books, pamphlets and newspapers, I sometimes see myself as a professional of God's word. While performing my duties, I read the transcription of many Bible verses, correcting grammatical errors or misinterpretations. Sometimes, I fear becoming so familiar with the Bible verses that they will become meaningless and lose their effect on me.

Then I read touching messages, personal witnesses or original interpretations of the Bible; and I feel deeply moved. Resisting the transforming power of scripture is impossible for me—even when I am working and not in meditation.

I have found that throughout the years, my livelihood has become a constant devotional time. God finds me in the midst of words and letters and allows me to see beyond them. I do not need to worry, for God's word never loses its power.

Prayer: *Thank you, God, for your written word. Help us to find joy in reading scripture. Amen*

Thought for the day: The precepts of the Lord are right, giving joy to the heart (Psalm 19:8).

Hideide Brito Torres (Minas Gerais, Brazil)

PRAYER FOCUS: THOSE WHO WORK IN PUBLISHING

SUNDAY 3 JULY

'How Does Jesus Do It?'

Read Isaiah 41:8–10, 17–20
The Lord says, 'Do not fear, for I am with you, do not be afraid, for I am your God; I will strengthen you, I will help you, I will uphold you with my victorious right hand.'
Isaiah 41:10 (NRSV)

About ten years ago, my beloved grandmother, Nan, was dying of cancer. We were grateful that her suffering was brief and that she died at home surrounded by her family. Nan had spent most of her life caring for others, and her children and grandchildren were her greatest joys. We were honoured to be there for her in her final moments.

I learned after Nan died that my dad had been praying for Christ to wrap his arms around Nan. He wanted her to be comforted, freed from her pain. He later told me that he knew the Lord had answered his prayer very clearly when Nan said to him, 'I don't know how he does it. I don't know how Jesus keeps me so warm!' My dad knew then that the Lord was telling him, 'I heard your prayer.'

As faithful followers of Christ, in times of despair we sometimes need consoling and a reminder that God's promise to care for us is still real. God does hear us and responds to us. I think back to my dad's prayer and to the Lord's answer through Nan. This experience is a reminder to listen and look for the messages that remind us that God's love and care for us never end.

Prayer: *Dear Lord, help us to look and listen for you in our lives. Help us to remember that you love us and care for us, especially in times of despair. Amen*

Thought for the day: God sends love and care when I need it most.

Lisa Gridley (Pennsylvania, US)

PRAYER FOCUS: GRATITUDE FOR GOD'S CARE

MONDAY 4 JULY

Wait on the Lord

Read Psalm 62:1–12
Truly my soul waiteth upon God: from him cometh my salvation.
Psalm 62:1 (KJV)

I frequently find myself waiting: queuing at the supermarket, stuck in traffic, sitting in the doctor's waiting room. I spend a lot of time waiting, and it seems like time wasted. I'd rather be busy.

But not all waiting is wasted time. Passage after passage in scripture implores us to 'wait on the Lord'. The instruction is hard for me to take. Waiting seems trivial compared to being up and doing. But waiting on the Lord is essential to experiencing a vital Christian life.

When God calls on us to wait, it isn't time spent hanging around. Waiting on the Lord involves intentionality. For me, it begins with shutting out distractions and continues with meditating on a passage of scripture. I then petition the Lord for wisdom and guidance with the expectation that God will answer. Waiting on the Lord can be productive. God has promised us strength to meet life's challenges and to rise above difficulties (Isaiah 40:31). The Lord is patiently standing by, ready to engage us. We must come and wait to experience God's blessing.

Prayer: *Dear watchful and caring God, give us the will to take time from our busy schedules to be with you. Amen*

Thought for the day: Time spent waiting on the Lord is not wasted time.

Wayne Greenawalt (Illinois, US)

PRAYER FOCUS: BUSY PEOPLE

TUESDAY 5 JULY

Light in the Forest

Read John 1:1–5
No one after lighting a lamp puts it under the bushel basket, but on the lampstand, and it gives light to all in the house.
Matthew 5:15 (NRSV)

I walk around a small lake for exercise, usually about three circuits. The lake is surrounded by forest. The other day while walking along a particularly dense area of the forest, I noticed that the setting sun was filtering light through the trees, creating stunning patches of colour. Different branches were bursting with oranges, reds and gold. It was quite a beautiful sight. But as I circled around the lake again, the colours were completely gone. In that period of about 15 minutes, the forest had gone totally dark. However, I still had that vivid image of colour in my mind.

It occurred to me that our faith in God can be like this experience. The Bible verse quoted above came to mind. The light of God is always there. Yet it sometimes seems to be dimmed or to go away entirely in times of struggle and pain. We might even be tempted to ignore it when things go wrong, but the light of God is always ready to burst with colour and energy and hope. Every time I walk by that particular section of forest, I think of that amazing light, and I give thanks that, though sometimes hard to see, God's light is always there.

Prayer: *O God, thank you for your light that is always shining, even when life seems hopeless. Amen*

Thought for the day: God's light is always shining.

Patricia M. Daniels (Florida, US)

PRAYER FOCUS: FOREST RANGERS

WEDNESDAY 6 JULY

Treasure Worth Passing On

Read Psalm 51:1–19
Here is a trustworthy saying: If we died with [Christ Jesus], we will also live with him; if we endure, we will also reign with him.
2 Timothy 2:11–12 (NIV)

As a child, my family situation was difficult, making it hard for me to trust God. Though I spent my whole life in the church, I remember rebellious days when I was either angry with God or ignored him. This was the result of my childhood pain, my insecurities, and my unwillingness to let God guide me. However, God did not ignore my situation. Despite everything I experienced, he remained faithful to me, helping me to realise that he was providing all the motivation I needed to restore my life.

Trusting God is one thing; faithfulness to God is another. Even King David, 'a man after [God's] own heart' (Acts 13:22), committed deep sins. But when he finally chose to confess his sins and repent, God gave him strength to save his kingdom and himself from all adversaries. David saw God's faithfulness, and so he chose to return to God and live faithfully.

Jesus is always ready to relieve us of the burden of sin. We, in turn, can resolve to be faithful and let God work in us and through us so that we can find new life in his service.

Prayer: *Dear God, help us to know that we can trust you to be with us and to guide us. Amen*

Thought for the day: Through Jesus Christ, God gives me the victory over death (see 1 Corinthians 15:57).

Kathleen Faye Dela Calzada (Philippines)

PRAYER FOCUS: CHILDREN WITH DIFFICULT HOME LIVES

THURSDAY 7 JULY

Love Song

Read Psalm 96:1–13

By day the Lord directs his love, at night his song is with me—a prayer to the God of my life.
Psalm 42:8 (NIV)

One Sunday afternoon, my wife and I had lunch at an Italian restaurant in our town. As we dined outside, a street musician strummed his guitar and sang love songs. His tenor voice, the lyrics and the harmonious blend of strings stirred my emotions.

While I was humming the words to one of the ballads, I was reminded that prayer is like a love song to God, and the Bible is full of songs to and about him. Some are called psalms and a number of them were composed when the psalmist was experiencing anguish, difficulties and stress. These prayerful songs remind us of our dependency on our sovereign God. In one psalm the author writes the poetic words of today's quoted verse. Singing praises to our God draws us into intimate worship. The psalms teach us that, at all times, we have reason to praise our Lord in prayer. We can continually remember God's faithfulness and active presence in our lives.

Prayer: *Dear God, you alone are worthy of our praise. Help us to find joy in praising you. Amen*

Thought for the day: Today I will sing to the Lord a new song (see Psalm 96:1).

Michael Lewis (Virginia, US)

PRAYER FOCUS: SINGERS

FRIDAY 8 JULY

Running the Race

Read Hebrews 12:1–3

[Let us fix] our eyes on Jesus, the pioneer and perfecter of our faith… so that [we] will not grow weary and lose heart.
Hebrews 12:2–3 (NIV)

Rejection letters are a normal part of my career as a writer. A seasoned writer once told me, 'When you have enough rejection letters to paper your wall, then you are a real writer.' The idea is that a 'real' writer doesn't give up but perseveres. A real writer keeps running the race.

Similarly, we are called to persevere in our faith. Hebrews 12:1 says that because we are surrounded by witnesses, we should throw off hindrances and besetting sins, running 'the race marked out for us'. Some of these witnesses are the great people of faith described in chapter 11 of Hebrews. Knowing the way in which they overcame obstacles and maintained their faith in God can help us not to grow weary or lose heart. We are often hindered and tempted to give up, yet we want to complete the task or mission God marked out for us.

We cannot overcome discouragement and persevere to the end by our own power. But we can focus on Jesus—on what we've learned about him through the Bible, Sunday school and church—and trust him. When we do this, Jesus will encourage us and guide us to do the work he has called us to do.

Prayer: *Thank you, Jesus, for your encouragement and for giving us strength to run the race set before us. Amen*

Thought for the day: Focusing on Jesus gives me the courage to persevere.

Judith Vander Wege (Iowa, US)

PRAYER FOCUS: THOSE DISCOURAGED IN THEIR WORK

SATURDAY 9 JULY

Cling and Grow

Read Luke 8:9–15

Make a tree good and its fruit will be good, or make a tree bad and its fruit will be bad, for a tree is recognised by its fruit.
Matthew 12:33 (NIV)

My friend Elizabeth can grow anything in her garden; she seems to have just the right touch. During a visit to her home, I marvelled at how the cucumber plants thrived under her care, so unlike my own puny harvest. When I looked at her vegetable patch, I noticed a high trellis. 'The plants need something to cling to,' Elizabeth explained. So that was it! While my plants floundered on the ground, hers climbed and spread.

Our Lord wants the same for us. God wants us to reach up and to spread out, multiplying his blessings. Like the cucumbers, we need something to cling to. Scripture provides us with the foundation we need: the ten commandments, the Lord's Prayer, the Beatitudes and much, much more. When we cling to the word—study it, commit it to memory and put it into practice—then we can freely share the good news by word and example.

Prayer: *Dear Lord, thank you for the gift of scripture. Help us to live by the word and to grow in your grace. Amen*

Thought for the day: We are nourished by God's word.

Monica A. Andermann (New York, US)

PRAYER FOCUS: FARMERS

SUNDAY 10 JULY

The Big Picture

Read Psalm 23
We know that in all things God works for the good of those who love him, who have been called according to his purpose.
Roman 8:28 (NIV)

Moving house is reckoned to be one of the most stressful happenings in life. But sometimes the aftermath is even more traumatic, as happened in my family, when a succession of difficulties made us ask if we had been right to move, and to question the above verse from Romans.

If we expect an easy life as followers of Christ, we are in for a shock! Jesus said it would be tough. There is distress as well as joy, fear as well as faith, doubt as well as hope. But whatever our circumstances, we can know the assured presence of God. He is faithful and constant in the hurly-burly of life.

In Psalm 23 David is content to trust God in every part of life—in green pastures and dark valleys—knowing that God's goodness and love will never fail.

We live each day with its ups and downs and see only a tiny part of God's big picture. We don't know what will happen tomorrow, but for today we can live with and for God, knowing that he works for our ultimate good. One day we will see the completed picture and realise how it all fitted together.

Prayer: *Thank you, Good Shepherd, for your presence each day. Help us to trust you and to be assured of your love and care in all circumstances. Amen*

Thought for the Day: I will not be afraid, for the Lord is with me.

Pam Pointer (Wiltshire, UK)

PRAYER FOCUS: THOSE MOVING HOUSE

MONDAY 11 JULY

Someone is Watching

Read James 1:22–25

Do not merely listen to the word, and so deceive yourselves. Do what it says.
James 1:22 (NIV)

Lillian and her husband were enjoying a quiet meal in a restaurant. Suddenly, they heard a man talking in a loud voice. The longer he talked, the louder his voice became. Evidently he wasn't pleased with his food or the service.

As he left the restaurant, the other diners could read on the back of his shirt the words of a Christian message. The words said one thing, but his actions conveyed a different message.

Years ago, I received a note in the morning mail. It was from a woman in our church, one who was a new Christian. She had written: 'I've watched you for a long time, not believing you were quite real. But now I have come to realise that you live what you say.' I hadn't realised that someone was watching to see if the way I lived matched the words I said.

It was a powerful reminder that when we take the name 'Christian', we also take on the responsibility of living as Christians, 24 hours a day, seven days a week.

Prayer: *Lord Jesus, help us to live our lives so that we always honour your holy name. Amen*

Thought for the day: Who is watching the way we live today?

Norma C. Mezoe (Indiana, US)

PRAYER FOCUS: RESTAURANT WORKERS

TUESDAY 12 JULY

Hide-and-Seek

Read Genesis 3:1–10

The man answered the Lord God, 'I heard you in the garden, and I was afraid… so I hid.'
Genesis 3:10 (NIV)

One of my favourite games as a child was hide-and-seek. Because I was small, I could fit into places bigger children could not reach. Because I could climb, I could perch high in the treetops while the other children searched for me below. I was convinced I was the best at hide-and-seek!

Years later I realised that my childhood success at hide-and-seek was directly related to my friends' lack of passion in looking for me. It's easy to hide, after all, when no one is seeking you.

At times in my life I have tried to hide from God. Bouts of rebellion have led me to places I thought he wouldn't go. I was like Adam and Eve cowering behind the trees or like Jonah fleeing to places I thought were beyond God's reach. Even when I was hiding, God was seeking a relationship with me with a passion I could not understand.

I think the psalmist described it best: 'If I go up to the heavens, you are there; if I make my bed in the depths, you are there… your right hand will hold me fast' (Psalm 139:8–10). God seeks each of us passionately.

Prayer: *Dear God, our companion, forgive us when we try to hide from you. Thank you for seeking us passionately. We pray in Jesus' name. Amen*

Thought for the day: God never stops seeking me.

Chuck Kralik (Missouri, US)

PRAYER FOCUS: SOMEONE WHO FEELS ABANDONED

WEDNESDAY 13 JULY

Willing To Help

Read 1 Corinthians 12:12–27
You are the body of Christ, and each one of you is a part of it.
1 Corinthians 12:27 (NIV)

In a church I was visiting while on holiday, an appeal went out for needleworkers to help mend the cloth used to cover the altar. As it wasn't my own church and I wasn't skilled at sewing, I didn't think it was my place to offer help. Nevertheless I was invited, so I went along.

When we started working, I discovered that this repair was actually a complete restoration of the altar cloth. The lady who had approached me had life-long experience on such projects in many of the cathedrals in our country. I did not have sewing experience, but they gave me a task. I spent the next couple of hours pulling out stray threads from the fabric with tweezers. Meanwhile, the experienced needleworkers were choosing fabrics, making a frame on which to work and sewing backing material to the frame—all under the expert's guidance.

Although I didn't have the skill for sewing, my work had saved the experienced sewers' time and effort. I was happy to be a part of this church's life, even in such a very small way. This experience showed me that God values our service—even when what we do seems insignificant. Each of us has a role to play in God's kingdom.

Prayer: *Dear God, help us to be willing to volunteer to help—even if we don't feel qualified for the task. Amen*

Thought for the day: Sometimes, all God asks for is my willingness to help.

Faith Ford (Hereford, England)

PRAYER FOCUS: WILLINGNESS TO WORK WHEREVER NEEDED

THURSDAY 14 JULY

Treading Water

Read Matthew 14:22–33

'Lord, if it's you,' Peter replied, 'tell me to come to you on the water.' 'Come,' [Jesus] said.
Matthew 14:28–29 (NIV)

I am not a strong swimmer. When I go in the sea, I am afraid of currents I cannot see, but I know from experience it will only make me exhausted to swim against the current. The sea becomes peaceful and enjoyable when I sense where the current is taking me and I allow it to move me in a direction where I can gradually reach the shore.

The same is true of God's will. There may be times when we struggle, and we may not be able to sense where he is guiding us. Whenever I read today's story, I am struck by the fact that the disciples struggled on their own for hours before seeing Jesus approaching them. I am reminded of the many storms in life where I have struggled, seemingly on my own, without placing my trust and confidence in the Lord. When I reached out to him, the peace came, often long before the storm subsided.

Like Peter, we can reach out to the Lord for help. We may have to wait, but peace comes to us when we come to him. Just as Jesus helped Peter on the water, when our confidence fails, Jesus will reach out and pull us up.

Prayer: *Dear God, our helper, remind us to come to you when we face struggles and storms, and bring us peace. Amen*

Thought for the day: Jesus helps me through the storms of life.

Mark H. Anderson (Pennsylvania, US)

PRAYER FOCUS: LIFEGUARDS

FRIDAY 15 JULY

Facing Mortality

Read 1 Corinthians 15:39–57
This perishable body puts on imperishability, and this mortal body puts on immortality.
1 Corinthians 15:53 (NRSV)

When the oncologist confirmed a diagnosis of prostate cancer, I felt devastated, disoriented, alone and helpless. As a minister, I had preached sermons on grief and led many discussions on the topic of grief, stress and depression. This was different. I was experiencing grief about my life, facing my mortality. My response was to request prayer. I also contacted my supervisor minister, and he arranged for me to receive anointing with oil. My devotional readings included *The Upper Room*, psalms and 1 Corinthians 13 and 15.

After surgery and chemotherapy, the cancer has not returned. Though not all my worry is gone, I dwell more on faith, hope and love than I do on the fact of my mortality.

Through my experience with cancer, I have come to believe in spiritual healing, even though spiritual healing may not necessarily result in physical healing or an extension of life. Prayers, medical care, love and healing by the Holy Spirit have given me a second chance to share the gifts of this life with my family, friends and many others who have spiritual and physical needs. No matter what our circumstances are, faith in Christ gives us each the promise of new life.

Prayer: *Dear God, help us face our own mortality and accept your promise of new life in you. Amen*

Thought for the day: When I trust in Christ, I can face my fears.

Don Coleman (West Virginia, US)

PRAYER FOCUS: CANCER PATIENTS

SATURDAY 16 JULY

Mobile Christianity

Read Matthew 28:16–20

[Jesus said], 'Go and make disciples of all nations, baptising them in the name of the Father and of the Son and of the Holy Spirit, and teaching them to obey everything I have commanded you.'
Matthew 28:19–20 (NIV)

In Jamaica, there are more phones per capita than in most parts of the world, despite our struggling economy. Our people believe in being connected to one another and are willing to pay more for their mobile phone contracts to ensure that they maintain this connection.

One Sunday, a lay preacher in our church used the analogy of the landline phone versus the mobile phone. He suggested that many of us are landline Christians; we only live our faith fully within the vicinity of our homes. The mobile phone goes everywhere with us. It has various features that can be used to connect with others. We can take it to work, to school, the shops, everywhere. And that is what Jesus expects us to do as Christians—to be mobile and share our faith with everyone, everywhere.

Jesus travelled widely, teaching and encouraging those he met to love one another. If he had remained in one location, the gospel may not have spread to those in need. Let us all strive to be mobile Christians to spread the word to every place we go.

Prayer: *Dear God, help us to share our love for you with everyone we meet, wherever we go. Amen*

Thought for the day: Am I a landline Christian or a mobile Christian?

Leila Vaughn (Jamaica)

SUNDAY 17 JULY

Let It Be

Read Isaiah 12:1–6
I will trust and not be afraid.
Isaiah 12:2 (NIV)

The song 'Let It Be', written in 1970 by Paul McCartney, has always brought me comfort. The song has become a new reminder in my life as I age. I am 88 years old, and am often aware that I am not able to do all the things I once could. I was reminded of this almost daily as our family gathered for a holiday together this June.

Through the years, I have been responsible for organising the holiday and doing the cooking. I enjoyed doing it and took pride in what I did to make the holiday a success. This time, however, it became obvious that I was no longer able to do what I had done in the past. This was difficult for me to accept. Again and again my children said, 'Dad, you have done a wonderful job, but now it's our turn. Let it be!'

All my working life, I served as a minister of local churches. How many times had I said to someone dealing with a difficulty: 'We are called to trust God and not be afraid'? I tried to reassure them in my own words, 'There will be an answer; let it be'.

But now it is me and my life! Faced with circumstances that I have not faced before, it is time to put my trust to the test. I have discovered in new ways that the promises of God are true. And day by day God is enabling me to 'let it be' in hands that are much more capable and caring than mine.

Prayer: *Dear God, teach us to let go and to trust you for all of the future you give us. Amen*

Thought for the day: What new responsibility is God calling me to take on?

David F. Knecht (North Dakota, US)

PRAYER FOCUS: FAMILY MEMBERS WITH NEW RESPONSIBILITIES

MONDAY 18 JULY

Food for the Soul

Read John 6:41–51
Jesus said, 'I am the bread of life.'
John 6:48 (NRSV)

Every time I hear the phrase 'the bread of life', I think of my grandparents' home in Ohio. With our family gathered around the table, my grandfather's blessing always ended with, 'Now bless this food to our bodies, and feed our souls with the bread of life.'

As a child, I always wondered what Jesus had to do with bread. The bread I knew came in a wrapper from the shop. Later, as a young wife and mother, I baked my own bread for several years. I can still feel the warm dough in my hands and wonder at the mystery of the yeast as it expanded my small lump of dough into a delicious loaf of bread. But Jesus as the bread of life? Looking back now over many years of my faith journey, I am aware of times when I have cried out to Jesus for help and he has kept me moving through each transition, doubt or loss. His words of love and forgiveness have nourished my battered soul more times than I can count.

That's the connection, isn't it? Just as earthly bread fills and nourishes our bodies, Jesus fills and nourishes our souls. That's what my grandfather meant when he prayed 'and feed our souls with the bread of life'.

Prayer: *Source of strength, thank you for feeding our bodies with the good things of the earth and our souls with your bountiful love and promise of salvation. Amen*

Thought for the day: Jesus is our bread for the journey.

Nancy J. Clark (Michigan, US)

PRAYER FOCUS: BAKERS

TUESDAY 19 JULY

Bleached Bright

Read Mark 9:2–13
There he was transfigured before them. His clothes became dazzling white, whiter than anyone in the world could bleach them.
Mark 9:2–3 (NIV)

My great-grandmother Eliza Jane emigrated from Ireland in 1888. She had five children, but only two lived to adulthood. In 1901, her husband, James, died of smallpox. Life was difficult for Eliza Jane. The only work she could find to support herself and her children was housework—washing clothes, cleaning windows, mopping floors, beating rugs—for wealthy families. My Aunt Margaret, her eldest child, said that no one anywhere could bleach sheets and linens like Eliza Jane. When she cleaned and bleached white sheets, they were almost too bright to look at.

When I read the story of Jesus' transfiguration, I think of Eliza Jane. Jesus is on the mountain with his dearest friends. Jesus' appearance and clothing are changed; he glows in glorious light—almost too bright to look at. And God speaks out of a cloud, affirming the Father's love for Jesus.

When we spend time studying scripture, a noticeable change comes over us as well. God's love can shine through our troubles, and we can carry that assurance to others by sharing our experiences of God's transforming love.

Prayer: *Lord Jesus, make us bright with the light of your love and compassion so that we may share your love with others. Amen*

Thought for the day: God's love makes us light for the world.

John Fischer (Washington, US)

PRAYER FOCUS: SOMEONE WHO CLEANS HOUSES FOR A LIVING

WEDNESDAY 20 JULY

Special Every Day

Read Ecclesiastes 3:1–8

You changed my mourning into dancing. You took off my funeral clothes and dressed me up in joy.
Psalm 30:11 (CEB)

Several years ago, when I replaced my worn, tattered Bible with a new one, I decided to try something new. Every day that I read a passage in *The Upper Room*, I marked the passage and wrote the date in the margin of my Bible. When the passage was especially meaningful or helpful to me, I also picked out a single verse and underlined it.

Five years later, I see by the dates that I have read the same passages several times. When I do my daily reading, I also think about the events that happened on those dates. Some dates fell before the birth of my son. Others were during a health crisis, while on maternity leave or during times of worry or stress.

I love reflecting on the highs and lows of my daily life and knowing that God's word has sustained me through them all. The phases of my life and my daily concerns have changed and affected what I have appreciated most from each reading. No matter what I was experiencing at the time, I could find meaning and draw strength from scripture. I am grateful to have God's word available to bless me in all the phases of my life.

Whether we are happy, sad, grateful, worried, ill or at peace, God speaks to us. Thanks be to God!

Prayer: *Thank you, God, for speaking to us through scripture. Give us grace to appreciate your guidance in our lives. Amen*

Thought for the day: Reflecting on the past gives me hope for God's blessings in the future.

Marney White (Connecticut, US)

PRAYER FOCUS: SOMEONE STARTING A NEW DISCIPLINE OF BIBLE STUDY

THURSDAY 21 JULY

Starting Over

Read Matthew 4:18–22
'Come, follow me,' Jesus said, 'and I will send you out to fish for people.'
Matthew 4:19 (NIV)

Whenever we start over again, whether it's a new career or a new way of life, we need to invest a great deal of time and attention if our new path is to be successful.

Jesus Christ offers all a new start, with a special invitation to leave behind our investment in worldly cares and follow him. Jesus gave this same invitation to his first disciples, Simon and Andrew, who were fishermen. 'Come, follow me,' Jesus said, 'and I will send you out to fish for people.'

I remember the Lord calling me in much the same way. I was beginning to realise that I could not handle my life by myself; I needed some faithful companion who would support me in both good days and bad. It was then that God called me—through my students, who invited me to their home and told me about Jesus, the companion I so greatly needed. From then on I have invested my time and attention in God's kingdom. I am trying to share the good news of God's love with those who need desperately to hear it.

With Christ as our companion, we can throw our nets in new directions, and with deep dedication begin or continue our special calling to fish for people by living lives of compassion and love.

Prayer: *Dear God, make us true disciples. Teach us to invest who we are and what we have for the good of your people everywhere. Thank you for inviting us into your kingdom. Amen*

Thought for the day: New life in Christ means new commitment.

Ratna Chapagain (Kathmandu, Nepal)

PRAYER FOCUS: THOSE TRYING TO MAKE A NEW START

FRIDAY 22 JULY

A Solace for the Soul

Read Exodus 14:5–14

When I am afraid, I put my trust in you.
Psalm 56:3 (NRSV)

Over 50 years ago I memorised my first Bible verse, Psalm 56:3, at Sunday school. The teacher told our small group of children that when we were afraid, it was very important to trust God because he cares about us.

It was not until many years later that I began to learn the true meaning of this powerful psalm. As new parents, my husband and I observed that our first child's hands and legs seemed to move abnormally on occasion, and we made an appointment with our paediatrician. I was afraid to know the diagnosis and afraid not to know it. I was afraid of our lack of experience as parents and afraid that what might lie ahead would need the expert experience of seasoned parents. Fear began to overwhelm me. But then I remembered that first Bible verse I had learned so many years ago: 'When I am afraid, I put my trust in you' (Psalm 56:3).

We may be afraid of many things: health issues, financial concerns, giving birth or approaching death. Whatever it may be, we can pray this psalm and allow it to flow through our souls, bringing peace. God can be trusted in all situations and with all our concerns.

Prayer: *Heavenly Father, thank you for peace that overflows my soul when I trust in you. Amen*

Thought for the day: In uncertain times, I can rely on scripture to comfort me.

Le-Ann Splawn Little (Alabama, US)

PRAYER FOCUS: PARENTS AWAITING A CHILD'S DIAGNOSIS

SATURDAY 23 JULY

God's Ways

Read Galatians 6:7–10
Many plans are in a person's mind, but the Lord's purpose will succeed.
Proverbs 19:21 (CEB)

As I waited for the shop assistant to find my order form, I felt frustrated that my day was slipping away. I still had many things to do within a limited time. Then a little voice within me said, 'Why don't you pray for the people around you?' I stopped glancing at my watch and noticed the nearby shoppers. Some seemed stressed; others were anxious or frustrated. I started praying for the people who passed by and smiled at those who looked my way. Finally, the assistant returned, apologetic that she couldn't find my order. 'That's OK,' I said. Instead of feeling frustrated or stressed, I felt peaceful, assured that I had used my time in the way God wanted. In order to do that, I had to relinquish my own agenda. Later in the day, I did the things I had to do without the slightest stress or hurry.

Now, when I wait, whether for a traffic light to change or for family members to get ready, I can relax and pray for the people around me. I feel the joy and excitement of being ready for whatever God has in store for me.

Prayer: *Thank you, God, for unexpected opportunities to connect with you. May we never be too busy to listen and to follow. Amen*

Thought for the day: Today I will pay attention to God's leading to pray for others.

Donna H. Eliason (Washington, US)

PRAYER FOCUS: SHOP ASSISTANTS

SUNDAY 24 JULY

Divine Potter

Read Jeremiah 18:1–11

The Lord said to Jeremiah, 'Like clay in the potter's hand, so are you in mine, house of Israel!'
Jeremiah 18:6 (CEB)

In the creation account found in Genesis 2, God creates humanity from the clay of the earth and breathes into humankind the breath of life. God is the creator and sustainer of all life, and we have within us his image and breath.

In the book of Jeremiah, God calls Jeremiah to the potter's house where Jeremiah finds a potter working at his wheel. The potter takes a spoiled vessel and reworks it into another vessel. 'Then the word of the Lord came to [Jeremiah]: "Can I not do with you… just as this potter has done?" says the Lord. "Just like the clay in the potter's hand, so are you in my hand."' Here again, with the image of clay, God gives us a powerful message: 'Can I not do with you… just as this potter has done?'

We are God's good creation—but we aren't always good! No matter how often we become cracked or marred, in God's hands we can become beautiful again as he shapes, moulds and recreates us in the divine image.

Prayer: *Loving God, mould our lives in such a way that we reflect the beautiful creation you desire us to be. Amen*

Thought for the day: I am made in the image of God.

Christopher Yopp (Virginia, US)

PRAYER FOCUS: CRAFTSMEN AND WOMEN

MONDAY 25 JULY

Calmed by God's Word

Read Psalm 46:1–11

God is our refuge and strength, an ever-present help in trouble.
Psalm 46:1 (NIV)

After attending an intensive training course for a week, I was anxious to get home. With traffic backed up on the motorway, however, I had to find a different route.

On the way, I discovered that my thoughts quieted. I began to consider the way God cares for us. As I drove along the alternative route, I began to see wonderful new sights. I rounded a bend in the road and saw a sparkling blue river that wound between cliffs and disappeared toward the horizon. I pondered how God calls us to be still even in the midst of trouble. I remembered Bible verses that help us to put aside our jumbled thoughts and to fix our minds on God's presence and promises.

When we make a habit of reading the Bible, memorising it and recalling it, the reassuring words of God can replace our worries.

They are always close at hand when we need comfort or assurance in our daily lives.

Prayer: *Dear Lord, help us to recall your words so that we can trust you to ease our anxieties. Thank you for your loving care. We pray as Jesus taught us, saying, 'Our Father in heaven, hallowed be your name, your kingdom come, your will be done, on earth as it is in heaven. Give us today our daily bread. And forgive us our debts, as we also have forgiven our debtors. And lead us not into temptation, but deliver us from the evil one.'* Amen*

Thought for the day: Daily Bible reading helps me remember God's presence.

Linda Jo Reed (Washington, US)

PRAYER FOCUS: THOSE TRAVELLING FOR WORK
* Matthew 6:9–13 (NIV)

TUESDAY 26 JULY

Bringing the Giants Down

Read 1 Samuel 17:31–37

David said, 'The Lord, who saved me from the paw of the lion and from the paw of the bear, will save me from the hand of this Philistine.'
1 Samuel 17:37 (NRSV)

David was a young lad whose job was to protect his flock of sheep from predators. He wasn't a mighty warrior, but what he lacked in size he made up in faith. Now he was ready to face the biggest challenge of his life so far—a giant. David didn't cower in his presence; he was ready to fight Goliath face-to-face with only a sling shot and a few smooth stones. He didn't need anything else because God was there in the fight with him.

We all face challenges. Some are small, and we easily work through them. Others become more difficult and life-altering until we face what seems like a gigantic obstacle. But we can stand firm and face it because God is with us.

No matter what giants we face—unemployment, health issues, the loss of a loved one—if we turn it over to God, we may overcome the obstacle in an unexpected way. God helped David defeat Goliath with a few smooth stones, and he can show us how to overcome our difficult situations and be victorious.

Prayer: *Heavenly Father, give us courage and strength. Help us to trust you as we face overwhelming obstacles. Amen*

Thought for the day: I can face any obstacle with God's help.

Christine Henderson (Texas, US)

PRAYER FOCUS: SOMEONE FACING AN OVERWHELMING OBSTACLE

WEDNESDAY 27 JULY

'I'm Having Fun!'

Read Psalm 100:1–5

Let everything that breathes praise the Lord!
Psalm 150:6 (NRSV)

I was working in Malaysia, and my parents were missionaries in Sierra Leone—in their last posting before retirement. Then I received news from my father that my mother had Dengue fever and was not expected to live. Her last message to my sisters and me was, 'Tell everyone that I am having fun!' Then, in the mission hospital, she passed into eternal life.

To some, those last words might seem strange. But I knew that my mother's faith led her to look ahead with spiritual excitement. My mother spent most of her life serving as a nurse in a Methodist Mission in Sierra Leone. She had always lived her life with great passion and faithfulness, and her final message showed me that she was looking forward with eager anticipation to life in heaven.

As Christians we are filled by the Holy Spirit, who gives us passion to serve others. Our life on earth is an adventure, and it's exciting because we have Jesus as the Lord of our life. Our faith gives us the certainty that even when sadness overtakes us, all will be well because of the love of Jesus.

Following my mother's example, we can find joy in allowing the Holy Spirit to lead us in serving others. We can also look forward with faithful anticipation to our heavenly future.

Prayer: *O God, show us the excitement we can have when we follow your will. Lead us through this life to life eternal. In Jesus' name. Amen*

Thought for the day: Christian living is an adventure with Christ.

Paul Juby (Norfolk, England)

PRAYER FOCUS: MISSIONARIES IN AFRICA

THURSDAY 28 JULY

Looking for God

Read Numbers 13:26—14:9

[Then Caleb said,] 'We can certainly do it.'
Numbers 13:30 (NIV)

When Moses sent twelve spies to see a land God had promised to give to the Israelites, the scouts came back with a unanimous report about what they had seen: the land flowed with milk and honey but formidable people guarded it.

Ten of the spies concluded they should give up all plans to possess a place filled with such intimidating people. But Caleb and Joshua argued that they should enter this bountiful land according to God's promise. Had these two missed something? What about the guards in their daunting strongholds? It was the ten, not Caleb and Joshua, who missed something. The ten failed to see God in the picture, while Caleb and Joshua pictured God shaping the outcome. They recalled God's past actions and trusted his promises for the future.

Global problems and personal challenges often demand our attention. But, like the ten spies, we often fail to see his presence in those circumstances. When we look for God in the picture, we can see things more clearly. We can step confidently into the future—however alarming it looks—and trust the Good Shepherd to lead the way.

Prayer: *Dear Lord, when horizons before us seem overwhelming, fill us with confidence in you. In Jesus' name. Amen*

Thought for the day: Today I will remember God's past faithfulness to me.

Cynthia Widmer (New York, US)

PRAYER FOCUS: PEACE IN OUR WORLD

FRIDAY 29 JULY

Standing Stronger

Read Psalm 71:19–21
You, who have shown me many troubles and calamities, will revive me once more. From the depths of the earth, you will raise me up one more time.
Psalm 71:20 (CEB)

Glancing out of the window that overlooks my garden, I was mesmerised by the steady stream of rain pouring down over the greenery and flowers. The thicker, sturdier leaves seemed to push up against the rain. But the delicate blossoms jerked this way and that, seeming to fight the raindrops that slapped against their petals. Their stems drooped as the rain persisted.

When the rain finally stopped, the sun broke through, and its warmth began evaporating the moisture. The delicate flowers seemed to shake off their heaviness and return to their strong upright position with even greater beauty.

We all experience the storms of life. Sometimes we are strong in the face of such trials; other times we feel weak under the weight of life's lessons. God always knows when we are unsteady and in need of divine strength. We can show this same kindness to others. Though we don't always know the extent of others' trials, we can always offer encouragement. We can offer our loving support and help others to stand a little stronger after the storm.

Prayer: *Heavenly Father, help us comfort others with the strength you give us. Amen*

Thought for the day: Whom is God calling me to encourage today?

Rita J. Flower-Opdycke (Florida, US)

PRAYER FOCUS: COMMUNITIES SUFFERING DROUGHT

SATURDAY 30 JULY

Longing for God

Read Psalm 42:1–11

As a deer longs for flowing streams, so my soul longs for you, O God. My soul thirsts for God, for the living God.
Psalm 42:1–2 (NRSV)

The corça is a small deer. As a desert animal, the corça has a sensitive sense of smell that enables it to smell water from miles away. It is able to detect water several feet below the ground. However, when the corça finds a source of water it does not stay there for an extended period of time; it keeps moving. When it is thirsty again, the corça has to seek other places where it can quench its thirst.

Sometimes we can become too comfortable with daily life. We think everything is fine, but if we do not seek God in new ways, we may miss opportunities to continue to grow in our faith. We may miss experiences and lessons we only learn in communion with God, by drinking from the Living Water (see John 4:14).

Just as the corça constantly seeks fresh water, we can leave the comfort zone of our spiritual life and seek to grow in the knowledge and grace of our Lord Jesus, expressing each day our longing for God.

Prayer: *Dear God, remind us to seek you in new places and never to grow complacent in our longing for you. Renew us with your living water, through Jesus Christ. Amen*

Thought for the day: How can I seek God in new ways today?

Francisco de Castro Maria (Luanda, Angola)

PRAYER FOCUS: THOSE WITHOUT ACCESS TO CLEAN WATER

SUNDAY 31 JULY

One Door Closes

Read James 5:13–18

Rejoice always, pray without ceasing, give thanks in all circumstances; for this is the will of God in Christ Jesus for you.
1 Thessalonians 5:16–18 (NRSV)

My friend Doris, an artist, was diagnosed with Parkinson's disease. She was gravely discouraged and all her friends also mourned. No longer could Doris provide portraits and beautiful paintings of waterfalls and sunsets. In desperation, Doris cried out, 'God, what good am I to anyone?'

Within a week someone from the local college called Doris to ask if she would teach a painting class. Students blossomed under her skilled instruction, and Doris was asked to return the following term.

Scripture invites us to pray about every aspect of our lives: the sufferings, the joys, the conflicts, even the weather. God hears and answers our prayers—rarely in predictable ways, but he answers all the same. How grateful we are for God, who cares about our challenges and our victories more than we do!

Prayer: *O God, give us grace to accept new opportunities. Amen*

Thought for the day: God often answers prayers in unexpected ways.

Barbara Christwitz (California, US)

PRAYER FOCUS: THOSE WITH PARKINSON'S DISEASE

MONDAY 1 AUGUST

From the Inside Out

Read 2 Corinthians 4:16–18

Create in me a clean heart, O God; and renew a right spirit within me.
Psalm 51:10 (KJV)

In the world of musical instruments, the trombone's warm, rich sound is beyond compare—in my opinion, of course! With proper care, a trombone can last a lifetime. Recently, I acquired a neglected trombone that had developed red rot, a corrosion that eats the brass away from the inside. When the corrosion breaks the surface, the trombone must be discarded because the damage cannot be repaired.

While unaffected by red rot, our human bodies are susceptible to a variety of ailments—and sooner or later, we all discover how vulnerable our bodies are. But the apostle Paul tells us that though our bodies may waste away, our spirits are continually renewed. Through Bible study, daily prayer and a desire to please God, we cultivate lives of faithfulness and obedience. When we nourish the spirit, we can find eternal life. When we neglect the spirit, it may become 'corroded' by the ways of the world.

There is no hope for a corroded trombone. But when our spirit becomes 'corroded', we need not despair. God promises forgiveness if we confess our sins with repentant hearts. He can restore our spirits and renew us (see 1 John 1:9).

Prayer: *Dear Lord, thank you for your grace and loving-kindness. Help us to care for our spirits by spending time daily with you. Amen*

Thought for the day: God renews my spirit each day.

Jacob Schneider (Maryland, US)

PRAYER FOCUS: MUSICIANS

TUESDAY 2 AUGUST

Never Alone

Read Isaiah 53:1–6

He took up our pain and bore our suffering, yet we considered him punished by God, stricken by him, and afflicted.
Isaiah 53:4 (NIV)

When my daughter was young, she was diagnosed with scoliosis (a sideways curvature of the spine). She was fitted with a hard plastic back brace, which she had to wear at all times. Often she would wake up at night crying in pain. When I talked to the doctor, he said that scoliosis does not cause the kind of pain my daughter was experiencing. We did not know what to make of her complaints or understand the severity of her pain.

Several years later I was diagnosed with cervical stenosis and degenerative disc disease. It was not until I was dealing with my own pain that I was able to understand my daughter's pain and I apologised to her for not understanding her suffering.

Just as I was able to better understand my daughter's pain because of my own, I am strengthened knowing that God understands my pain because he was wrapped in human flesh. Jesus therefore understands our suffering, grief and loss. In all our trials, our Saviour is with us. When others are suffering, we can share the good news that we do not go through it alone. Our God suffers with us.

Prayer: *Gracious God, help us to identify with others and to seek to be Christ to those who are suffering. Remind us that you are with us through every trial. Amen*

Thought for the day: How do I recognise the presence of God in my pain?

Jacqui Rose-Tucker (Georgia, US)

PRAYER FOCUS: THOSE WITH SPINAL DISEASE

WEDNESDAY 3 AUGUST

Welcoming Strangers

Read Leviticus 19:32–37

I was a stranger and you invited me in.
Matthew 25:35 (NIV)

Walking down the street in my home town I see many recent arrivals to the United Kingdom. They do not speak our language well; they have their own ways and customs. Many local people say, 'Why are these people here? Why can't they stay in their own countries?'

My friend, once a missionary in a country where it is illegal to preach the gospel, suggested that we view their presence among us as a God-given opportunity to befriend new people and lead them to faith in Christ.

The people of Israel were commanded to treat the stranger in their midst as one born among them. Do we? Jesus, as a young child, was a refugee in Egypt. Would we have welcomed his family?

Our church started a weekly English language class some years ago, and many people continue to attend and form connections. New people come to church events, and some are coming to faith in Christ. When we obey the Lord we can accept the stranger as we would like to be accepted.

Prayer: *Dear Lord, open our hearts to welcome the strangers among us. Amen*

Thought for the day: Whom will I welcome in Christ's name today?

Marion Turnbull (Merseyside, England)

THURSDAY 4 AUGUST

Shaping Your Life

Read Romans 12:1–2
Never be lacking in zeal, but keep your spiritual fervour, serving the Lord.
Romans 12:11 (NIV)

I attend an exercise class three times a week. I spend time doing aerobics and lift weights for muscle tone and strength. Some of the exercises are difficult to execute in the way our leader expects; I have difficulty in holding weights at arm's length. I cannot quite do some of the stretching exercises. I am improving, but without spending time concentrating and working on these exercises, I do not get the full benefit of the workout.

The same principle is true of the spiritual life. I strive to strengthen my faith through intentional practice by studying the Bible and reading Christian books. I try to be conscious of my surroundings and look for opportunities to witness to God's love through my actions. I regularly attend church and a Bible study group. I read the Bible and a daily devotional book every morning, comparing what I read and hear with my everyday life.

Even with practice, I sometimes struggle in my faith. Yet I am improving. As I spend more time studying and seeking to do God's work, I live more fully the life of discipleship I have chosen.

Prayer: *Steadfast God, help us to discern and to choose your will for our lives. Amen*

Thought for the day: I will shape my life with Christian study and action.

Ruben G. Garza (Texas, US)

PRAYER FOCUS: THOSE SEEKING A BETTER RELATIONSHIP WITH GOD

FRIDAY 5 AUGUST

Weeding Out Negativity

Read Mark 4:3–9

Whatever is true, whatever is noble, whatever is right, whatever is pure, whatever is lovely, whatever is admirable—if anything is excellent or praiseworthy—think about such things.
Philippians 4:8 (NIV)

After recent heavy rains, I was eager to get back to work in my garden. Not having to spend so much time watering had been a welcome relief during the heat of summer, and my plants were flourishing. The weeds prospered even more. They seemed to grow at twice the rate of the other plants, choking them in the process.

My mind is similar to my garden. Negative thoughts seem to crop up faster than the positive ones and threaten to overpower them. As I do with the weeds, I must be diligent in pulling out destructive thoughts by the roots before they take over my thinking.

I have found that the best way for me to weed my thoughts is to start each day focused on Bible reading and prayer. Setting my mind on God's truth first thing in the morning acts as a protective shield for me throughout the day. When negative thoughts arise, God's promises help me to recognise them and give me strength to remain focused on his truth.

Prayer: *Dear God, thank you for giving us your word of truth to lead us and to guide us in following your will. Amen*

Thought for the day: Staying focused on God's truth helps me to think clearly.

Sandee Story (North Carolina, US)

PRAYER FOCUS: GARDENERS

SATURDAY 6 AUGUST

Steadfast in Prayer

Read Luke 18:1–8
Pray in the Spirit at all times in every prayer and supplication. To that end keep alert and always persevere in supplication for all the saints.
Ephesians 6:18 (NRSV)

My mother's health was deteriorating due to pneumonia. Every night, we anticipated the worst. She coughed through the night, and her coughs were deep and terrifying. Her condition was complicated by the fact that she had hepatitis, diabetes and hypertension.

Yet her attitude amazed me. Instead of complaining, she spent her time engaged in fervent prayer. Every night, as the battle with a racking cough raged, she prayed for healing until one day, it came.

Our hearts were greatly encouraged by her healing and by the power of prayer. Today, four years later, my mother is still healed of pneumonia. She is able to sleep peacefully, cough-free, rejoicing in what God has done.

Paul reminds us in the verse quoted above to always persevere in prayer. Even though illness or other circumstances may bring devastation, when we pray persistently, God hears our prayers and surrounds us with love.

Prayer: *Healer of the sick, fan the flame of perseverance in prayer for all who are ill. Amen*

Thought for the day: I will be persistent in prayer.

Nwakuche Emeka (Lagos, Nigeria)

PRAYER FOCUS: THOSE WHO SUFFER FROM SERIOUS ILLNESS

SUNDAY 7 AUGUST

Chosen

Read Isaiah 43:1–7

The Lord says, 'Don't fear, for I have redeemed you; I have called you by name; you are mine.'
Isaiah 43:1 (CEB)

'We pick Lisa.' 'We want Debbie.' 'Susan.' 'Janice.' I listened as they called name after name, dividing my classmates into teams. Smiling girls ran to one side or the other, laughing and clapping their hands in excitement. Not me. Growing up, I failed at any and all sports. My inability to stay focused on the play matched my clumsiness. As a result, I was always among the last chosen.

Standing alone, waiting for a team leader to pick me, I felt the minutes drag by like hours. I wanted and needed acceptance. The day I left high school, part of my joy involved putting that pain behind me.

No matter what our experience is in school sports, none of us has to feel unwanted, abandoned or rejected because God has called our names. Inexplicably, God has chosen each of us for an all-star team. We don't require special skills to earn a place or need to stand on the sidelines waiting to be chosen. Before our birth, our Father selected us and will support us against every opponent, even sin and death. Blessed with the freedom of acceptance and secure in God's promise never to reject us, we can excel. We are beloved children of God, cheering one another on toward a final victory.

Prayer: *Heavenly Father, help us remember that you have chosen us for your team. Amen*

Thought for the day: Everyone belongs in God's team.

Heidi Gaul (Oregon, US)

PRAYER FOCUS: THOSE FEELING ABANDONED

MONDAY 8 AUGUST

Reflections

Read Philippians 4:4–9
Be still, and know that I am God.
Psalm 46:10 (NIV)

Before winter arrived, my wife and I went on a driving holiday. The colours of the autumn leaves were amazing. As we absorbed the beauty of God's creation, we began looking more carefully at the many small lakes along the side of the road. The reflections of the trees and hills in the areas of still waters were breathtaking.

The scriptures have much to say about how we need to reflect Christ to the world, to show him to the world by the lives we live. Over the years, I have often heard Christian friends express how difficult it is to do this in our busy world. Perhaps we can look again at the reflections on the water and understand that perfect reflections only occur in perfect stillness. If we want to know Christ better and reflect him to the world, we can start by being still and seeking the peace that passes all understanding in our hearts. In this way we will be better able to share that peace with the world.

Prayer: *Dear Lord, calm us so that we can find your peace for ourselves and then share it with others around us. Amen*

Thought for the day: How can I reflect Christ to the world each day?

Gavin Leverton (Western Cape, South Africa)

PRAYER FOCUS: TO SEEK CHRIST'S PEACE

TUESDAY 9 AUGUST

Through God's Power

Read Matthew 26:69–75

Jesus said, 'You are Peter, and on this rock I will build my church, and the gates of Hades will not overcome it.'
Matthew 16:18 (NIV)

Jesus told Peter he would be the 'rock', the foundation of Jesus' church. But we see throughout scripture that Peter had several weaknesses. He often spoke before he thought through a situation. He was very impulsive, abrupt in his actions and was also discourteous to those around him. Peter was the disciple who cut off the high priest's servant's ear as the men came to arrest Jesus in the garden of Gethsemane.

Peter said he would die before disowning Jesus. But, as Jesus predicted, Peter denied Jesus three times before the crucifixion.

Jesus was very aware of Peter's failures, yet he saw his true heart. Jesus knew Peter would go on to do great things for God's kingdom.

Like Peter, we have many shortcomings and frequently fail to live fully as disciples of Christ. However, when this happens, we must never think that God cannot use us. It is through God's strength and power that we can achieve all that we are called to do.

Prayer: *Dear Father, help us to remember that we can rely on your strength to accomplish what you call us to do. Amen*

Thought for the day: I can rely on God's strength today.

Carol Goodman Heizer (Kentucky, US)

PRAYER FOCUS: SOMEONE WHO FEELS UNWORTHY

WEDNESDAY 10 AUGUST

Do Something

Read Joshua 1:1–9

You shall meditate on it day and night, so that you may be careful to act in accordance with all that is written in it. For then you shall make your way prosperous, and then you shall be successful.
Joshua 1:8 (NRSV)

William and I were hospital chaplains. One day we shared our favourite scripture verses. His was Joshua 1:8. As we talked, he asked, 'Do you know why? It's the first Bible verse that made me do something. It made me want to memorise more Bible verses. It made me want to think and study God's word because I wanted to know more about God's prosperity and success.'

Initially I thought he was being selfish: prosperity and success in today's world often equates to having material things. But as I got to know William, I learned his life in Christ was rooted in scripture. He was reading the Bible almost every time I saw him and had hundreds of verses memorised. For William, Joshua 1:8 was not about finding worldly prosperity and success. William found God's prosperity and success in discipleship and devotion to scripture.

The same words that inspired my colleague inspired Joshua to lead God's people across the Jordan to the promised land. Memorising scripture so that we can rely on it day and night helps us to seek God's prosperity and success through discipleship. God's words inspire discipleship; they empower us to do something.

Prayer: *O God, awaken us to the joy of discipleship. Empower us through your word to do your work in the world. Amen*

Thought for the day: How will I be a disciple today?

Walt Garrett (Arkansas, US)

PRAYER FOCUS: HOSPITAL CHAPLAINS

THURSDAY 11 AUGUST

The Least of These

Read Matthew 25:34–40

Is it not [the fast I choose] to share your food with the hungry and to provide the poor wanderer with shelter?
Isaiah 58:7 (NIV)

Margarita grew up in the mountains, herding goats and living in a humble adobe dwelling with her seven siblings. At mealtime, her mother always placed an extra plate on the table. When asked why, her response was: 'It's for God.' One day a hungry traveller arrived and was invited to their table; they all understood their mother's teaching.

When she was older, Margarita went to the city to escape poverty, only to land in a homeless hostel, like many others before her. Margarita is now a social activist and does volunteer work at one of the hostels in Buenos Aires, which ministers to children and adults living in extreme poverty.

Through all these experiences, Margarita has continued to follow her mother's example, to live with compassion and do all things for God. The kingdom of God is built by people like Margarita. Following her example we can all be filled with the Holy Spirit and mirror the actions of Jesus to serve the 'least of these' (Matthew 25:40).

Prayer: *Dear God, give us vision to see your purposes and grace to follow where you lead. In the name of Christ Jesus, we pray. Amen*

Thought for the day: For whom does God call me to be an advocate today?

Hugo N. Urcola (Buenos Aires, Argentina)

PRAYER FOCUS: SOCIAL ACTIVISTS

FRIDAY 12 AUGUST

Rest for the Weary

Read Matthew 11:28–30

Praise be to the Lord, to God our Saviour, who daily bears our burdens.
Psalm 68:19 (NIV)

Last summer, a hailstorm damaged the roof of our house. When it was time to replace it, heavy bundles of roof tiles arrived. A lift hoisted the entire pallet to the roof, where several men unloaded the tiles and distributed them across the top. I asked my husband why the pallet couldn't be left in place in a single stack. 'Each bundle weighs about 70 pounds,' he said. 'If the pallet were left intact, the weight could compromise the integrity of the rafters. The load could come crashing through the ceiling.'

The weight of the pallet reminded me of the burdens I sometimes carry. Whether they are relational, financial, health-related or simply part of the busyness of everyday life, trying to deal with the issues alone is always overwhelming. It can weaken me and make me less productive.

Jesus reminds us that we don't have to struggle on our own with fears, worries or trials that weigh us down. He invites each of us to come to him when we are tired from carrying heavy burdens and promises that we will find rest. That's a promise we can always rely on.

Prayer: *Dear Lord, help us to cast our burdens on you and to remember how much you love us. Amen*

Thought for the day: God is always ready to share the weight of my burdens.

Marlene Briggs (South Dakota, US)

PRAYER FOCUS: THOSE WITHOUT SHELTER

SATURDAY 13 AUGUST

To be a Missionary

Read 1 Peter 4:12–16

If you suffer as a Christian, do not be ashamed, but praise God that you bear that name.
1 Peter 4:16 (NIV)

The word 'missionary' conjures up images of travelling to foreign countries to spread God's word, and I'm always inspired by letters from missionaries describing ways they serve God by serving the people around them.

However, we don't have to move to another country to be a missionary. I can be one by telling the good news in my own neighbourhood. With evangelism, the issue isn't where we are but our willingness to spread God's message. Do we have the faith to call on and believe in the Holy Spirit to help us face our fears, discomfort and insecurity about sharing the gospel of Jesus with others?

In the past, fear of rejection from my peers overwhelmed my sense of knowing—and sharing—who I am as a Christian. It was easier to back away from those situations than to face my discomfort boldly with the faith that the Holy Spirit would see me through. But I have discovered that prayer, Bible reading and a growing faith can prepare any of us to share the knowledge of Christ confidently—whether out in the wide, wide world or in our little corner of it.

Prayer: *Dear Father, forgive our hesitancy to talk to others about you. Help us to be bold in sharing your good news. Amen*

Thought for the day: My mission field is the one I'm standing in.

Margie Harding (Maryland, US)

PRAYER FOCUS: MISSIONARIES

SUNDAY 14 AUGUST

Great is Your Faithfulness

Read Lamentations 3:19–23

The steadfast love of the Lord never ceases, his mercies never come to an end; they are new every morning; great is your faithfulness.
Lamentations 3:22–23 (NRSV)

Sometimes I get discouraged by the responsibilities of work and family. I sometimes struggle to provide for my family. When I get discouraged, I often think of the prophet Jeremiah. Jeremiah spent his entire life in the service of God. He was called to prophesy the doom of Judah to a stubborn people who refused to listen and repent. It seemed a fruitless task that often brought Jeremiah verbal and physical abuse (see Jeremiah 11:19).

Toward the end of his long life, Jeremiah sat in the burning wreck of Jerusalem to reflect on his life and God's judgement of Judah. He had every right to complain. Instead, he praised God's faithfulness and mercies each and every morning! He rejected despair, even in the ruins of his city, and chose to place his hope in God (see Jeremiah 42). When I tend toward despair, I remember Jeremiah's great faith, and every morning I rise in prayer, thankful for my Creator's mercies and faithfulness!

Prayer: *Dear God, thank you for the mercies you give every morning. Help us to turn to you when we despair. Amen*

Thought for the day: Where have I seen God's faithfulness today?

Jim Weems (Mississippi, US)

PRAYER FOCUS: FAMILIES WITHOUT BASIC NECESSITIES

MONDAY 15 AUGUST

God's Prompting

Read Philippians 2:1–11
Whoever serves me must follow me. Wherever I am, there my servant will also be. My Father will honour whoever serves me.
John 12:26 (CEB)

Recently, during a meeting of our prayer group, our minister asked us to share our experience of accepting Christ as Saviour. Many in the group talked about dramatic experiences in their personal journeys: tears, laughter, strong renewal of the faith, hope for the future and above all an immediate transformation in their lives. Many also spoke of hearing God's voice.

I can honestly say that my experience was not as vivid or dramatic. In fact, I feel that God has never spoken to me directly.

However, I do know that God's prompting led me in a new direction when I felt a strong desire to serve people in need. Ever since, my focus has been on the elderly members of my congregation who are no longer able to prepare their own meals. I prepare meals for them several times a week. I find great satisfaction in this ministry and feel blessed to obey Christ's call to help our neighbours.

Prayer: *Loving God, we are grateful for the prompting of the Holy Spirit to help those in need. As Jesus taught us, we pray, 'Our Father which art in heaven, Hallowed be thy name. Thy kingdom come. Thy will be done, as in heaven, so in earth. Give us day by day our daily bread. And forgive us our sins; for we also forgive every one that is indebted to us. And lead us not into temptation; but deliver us from evil.'* Amen*

Thought for the day: I serve God when I serve my neighbour.

Ivette Rivera (Puerto Rico)

PRAYER FOCUS: FOOD BANKS

* Luke 11:2–4 (KJV).

TUESDAY 16 AUGUST

The Glory of the Lord

Read Psalm 19:1–5
The heavens declare the glory of God; the skies proclaim the work of his hands.
Psalm 19:1 (NIV)

One weekend, I decided to do one of my favourite things: take a sunrise bicycle ride. I love feeling the early morning air, seeing the dew on the grass, and hearing the birds singing. As I began my ride, I started to praise God for all the marvellous things he has done and created. Then I noticed the sun coming up over the horizon. I stopped for a few minutes to take in the glorious view and ponder the artistry of our Creator. How awesome that God creates views like this! The verse quoted above came to mind.

Often we are too busy to notice the creative work of God. We are so caught up in our daily routines and with the hustle and bustle of life that we do not stop for even a moment to take in what God has created—the heavens and the earth. When we slow down long enough to observe his handiwork, we will be filled with praise and be ready to live each day with a sense of awe at the glory of our God.

Prayer: *Dear God, thank you for creating the beautiful and majestic heavens and the earth to help us know you more deeply. Help us never forget to give the glory to you. Amen*

Thought for the day: Today I will praise God for the beauty of creation.

Todd Diedrich (Wisconsin, US)

PRAYER FOCUS: TO BE GOOD STEWARDS OF CREATION

WEDNESDAY 17 AUGUST

My All

Read Mark 12:41–44
Love the Lord your God with all your heart and with all your soul and with all your mind and with all your strength.
Mark 12:30 (NIV)

The widow in today's reading knew that even sacrifices that seem small to others can be painful. She carefully placed her money in the temple treasury. Did she wonder what good such a 'small' offering could do? Did she doubt if God would notice how much it truly cost?

Sometimes I wonder if God really cares about the little decisions we make. But when I read this story, I know that God notices what our sacrifices cost. When we offer him something as 'small' as thinking a holy thought when we want to be critical, wading through a trial with joy rather than bitterness or loving someone who irks us, God notices our attempt to honour and obey. However, the reverse is also true. God knows when what I 'sacrifice' costs me little.

I know that God forgives me when I do not invest in the lives of others, but I realise that this is not the best way to respond to his breathtaking, life-saving grace. Out of love, I want to serve God, not with just a little, not even with a lot, but with everything he has given me. God is worth my all!

Prayer: *Dear Lord, we want to offer you everything. Grant us opportunities to give you our all—all our heart, soul, mind and strength. Amen*

Thought for the day: What will I gladly sacrifice for God today?

Bliss Baird (Kansas, US)

PRAYER FOCUS: SOMEONE WHO HAS SACRIFICED FOR ME

THURSDAY 18 AUGUST

Change Happens

Read Isaiah 43:14–21

Peter replied, 'Change your hearts and lives.'
Acts 2:38 (CEB)

As a minister who moves to a new church at the direction of my bishop, I know how difficult change can be. New faces, new names, new ideas and learning new ways that people interact together are some of the challenges in each new location.

Receiving a new leader can be an uneasy transition for congregations as well. What will the new minister focus on? Will our mission focus need to change? Will our theological ideas differ?

As Jesus preached and taught, he called people to change their hearts, their old ways of living and thinking. Christ called those who heard his voice to live for God and for neighbour, and to not think so much about self.

We will all encounter change in our lives. We know that uneasiness, confusion and fear are often part of that. Whether change comes in our churches, families, work or relationships, we can know that Christ always walks with us through these changes. We are never abandoned; we are never alone. Changes we encounter can deepen our spiritual lives as we rely more fully on Christ.

Prayer: *Holy One, walk with us as our lives change. Help us to trust you daily as you guide our steps. In Jesus' name. Amen*

Thought for the day: Christ walks with me through every change.

Jerry W. Krueger (Ohio, US)

PRAYER FOCUS: CHURCHES RECEIVING A NEW MINISTER

FRIDAY 19 AUGUST

Darkness and Light

Read Genesis 1:14–19

The light shines in the darkness, and the darkness has not overcome it.
John 1:5 (NIV)

My mother was a teenager in Norway during World War II. She has told me what it was like to grow up in a country under siege. Among other things, she has mentioned how totally dark it was at night. Everyone had to darken their windows, and no streetlights were lit—to prevent enemy bombers from seeing their targets.

One evening, during a rather difficult period of my life, I was praying. Suddenly, I pictured a house situated in complete darkness, with all the blinds drawn but fully lit on the inside. Then the blinds were pulled aside, and the light streamed out into the darkness. But the darkness did not stream into the light!

This vision renewed my hope. The despair that had threatened to overwhelm me could not stand against the love of Jesus Christ. He is in me and he surrounds me. Life's struggles are unavoidable. But when we stay close to Jesus in all circumstances, we will be safe: 'Whether we live or die, we belong to the Lord' (Romans 14:8).

Prayer: *Thank you, Jesus, for carrying me through the hard days. Amen*

Thought for the day: Despair can never conquer the love of Christ.

Elin Ulmo Hunnes (Volda, Norway)

SATURDAY 20 AUGUST

Hinderers

Read Mark 2:1–5
And when they could not bring him to Jesus because of the crowd, they removed the roof above him; and… they let down the mat on which the paralytic lay.
Mark 2:4 (NRSV)

When Jesus is in Capernaum, four men know somebody who needs him, so they set out to get their friend to him. When they get to the house, they can't get in because of a crowd.

In this story, I see three groups of people. There is the man who can't walk. There are helpers—the men who are trying to get their friend to Jesus. And there are hinderers—the crowd. Those in the crowd did not mean to hinder the paralytic from meeting Jesus; many of them did not even realise they were preventing his approach.

How many times have we been like that crowd? The hungry need food. Prisoners need someone to visit them. My church needs volunteers. The list goes on. What am I doing? I often realise, too late, that I have even been hindering the process. I have learned that it takes our whole selves to be helpers and faithful workers for Christ. It takes our eyes and ears to recognise the needs around us; our hands and feet to get the job done; our hearts to recognise when we are being hinderers and to move us to compassion to provide care for those in need.

Prayer: *Dear Lord, make us instruments for your work. Help us to recognise the needs of others and serve you faithfully. Amen*

Thought for the day: I can be a helper or a hinderer. What will I be today?

Lynda Prevatt (Alabama, US)

PRAYER FOCUS: OUTREACH MINISTRIES IN MY CHURCH

SUNDAY 21 AUGUST

God is Working

Read Ephesians 2:1–10

Come and hear, all you who fear God, and I will tell what he has done for me.
Psalm 66:16 (NSRV)

Each Sunday, I enter worship in full command of my emotions. But it often doesn't last. A verse or phrase of a hymn I have sung for decades strikes me in an entirely new way. I reflect on how God has worked in my life, in the lives of my loved ones and in members of the church I attend. A flood of memories and feelings pour over me. I am overwhelmed with gratitude for God's grace and mercy, and tears come to my eyes.

For many years I could not have imagined standing in church, unashamed of my lack of composure. I could not have imagined being comfortable talking about my faith or praying in public. Then, through many different experiences, not all of them positive, God broke through my shell of insecurity and self-protection. He put agents of grace in my path, and opened my heart to their acceptance and love. When I finally understood that God is present and active in my life and the lives of others, I became more confident in my faith and more committed to grow in it.

Some may think of God as abstract and remote. But for me, the opposite is true. The Holy Spirit can transform the way we experience God, inviting us into a personal relationship with our Creator.

Prayer: *Gracious God, thank you for being with us each day. Grant us courage to respond to you. Amen*

Thought for the day: How has my response to God's grace changed over time?

Hayes Mizell (South Carolina, US)

MONDAY 22 AUGUST

God Answers Prayer

Read 2 Samuel 12:15-23
The Lord himself goes before you and will be with you; he will never leave you nor forsake you.
Deuteronomy 31:8 (NIV)

When my husband was critically ill, I prayed and fasted, asking God to heal him, but my husband died. At that moment I could not understand why God did not answer my prayer. But during my grieving moment a friend shared David's story in today's reading with me. I found strength in David's words when he said: 'Can I bring him back again? I shall go to him, but he will not return to me.'

God answers prayer but not always in the way we want or expect. In 2 Samuel, David's child is ill. David fasts and prays desperately so that the child will live, even when he knows that God has clearly said the child will die. David thought his prayer and fasting could change the outcome—but it did not. God did not heal David's child or my husband, but God remained present.

Losing a loved one is painful, but we can learn to move forward. We can take comfort in God's promise to Paul: 'My grace is sufficient for you, for my power is made perfect in weakness' (2 Corinthians 12:9). When we draw on God's grace day by day and allow him to heal our wounded soul, life will go on, and God will always be there for us.

Prayer: *Dear Lord, comfort us when we grieve and give us grace to move forward, knowing that you will be with us. Amen*

Thought for the day: Life goes on, and God goes with us.

Rhoda Gowarto Manzo (Gombe, Nigeria)

PRAYER FOCUS: SOMEONE WHOSE SPOUSE HAS DIED

TUESDAY 23 AUGUST

Coming Home

Read Luke 15:11–24

While he was still a long way off, his father saw him and was filled with compassion for him; he ran to his son, threw his arms around him and kissed him.
Luke 15:20 (NIV)

My wife and I went to the airport to pick up our daughter when she returned from visiting her grandmother. We waited in the long hallway where all the arriving passengers would eventually emerge. The numbers grew as people gathered and peered anxiously down the tiled tunnel hoping for a glimpse of their loved one.

Relief and excitement spread across faces as people spotted and greeted those for whom they had been waiting. Watchers abandoned their posts and rushed forward to joyous reunions. As we all walked back and forth excitedly waiting to spot our special person to know they were safely home, I thought about God's love for us.

I know that God watches and waits for us with the same longing. He longs to see, welcome and hold each of us. No one will ever love us with as much depth and intensity as Jesus, who gave himself for us on the cross. I rest assured knowing that if some sin, temptation or mistake has lured us into a 'far country' like the son in today's reading, the promise of forgiveness awaits us when we return to God's loving arms.

Prayer: *Dear God, thank you for families and friends who love us. Thank you for your love and presence in our earthly life and the promise that you will welcome us into our eternal home with you for ever. Amen*

Thought for the day: God is always ready to welcome me.

Joey Yow (North Carolina, US)

PRAYER FOCUS: THOSE WHO ARE SEPARATED FROM LOVED ONES

WEDNESDAY 24 AUGUST

Inner Peace

Read Psalm 139:1–12

Set me free from my prison [O Lord], that I may praise your name. Then the righteous will gather about me because of your goodness to me.
Psalm 142:7 (NIV)

I have recently formed a friendship with my friend's son, who is in prison. As I read his letters, I am often struck by his ability to look deeply into his life. In one letter he shared his thoughts on ways of keeping himself focused on positive things: communing with God and allowing God's word to uplift him, encourage him, and comfort him when he is having negative, self-defeating thoughts. Sometimes he includes some favourite scripture quotations.

I have learned from my friend's letters that our minds can be free no matter where we are—even in an uncomfortable place.

Conversely, we can be physically free to move about in search of peace, but our minds may not find true contentment. If we are honest, we can all admit to having some form of confinement that threatens our peace. But whether we are in prison or not, the message of Psalm 139 can bring us peace. Wherever we are, wherever we go, God is there. Those whom God sets free are free indeed!

Prayer: *O Lord, you are our shepherd, and we shall not want. Surely your goodness and mercy shall follow us all the days of our lives (see Psalm 23). We are eternally grateful. Amen*

Thought for the day: Because God has set me free, I am free indeed.

Sharon Owens-Davis (New Jersey, US)

PRAYER FOCUS: THOSE IN PRISON

THURSDAY 25 AUGUST

Gifts for Service

Read Exodus 35:30—36:1
Each of you should use whatever gift you have received to serve others, as faithful stewards of God's grace in its various forms.
1 Peter 4:10 (NIV)

I have been crocheting since I was a teenager. I enjoy the softness of the yarn as it glides through my fingers. I delight in the blending of the pinks, greens, blues and yellows as a baby blanket takes shape.

Over the years, I have given away many crocheted items as gifts; but until recently, I had not thought of using the skill as a ministry. Would God use crochet as a way to help reach others for the Lord? I searched for answers in the Bible, and found that during the time of Moses, God called skilled craftsmen to build the tabernacle. And God used Tabitha's skill of sewing to minister to others (Acts 9:39).

So I started a ministry at my church where we seek out areas of need in the community and crochet or knit items to help meet those needs. To each item we attach a card with Bible verses so that the receivers may be drawn to Christ.

If we allow God to do so, he can and will use whatever skills we have. I feel blessed to know that the scarves, hats and baby booties I crochet will help others to know the love of Jesus.

Prayer: *Thank you, God, for using our simple gifts to serve others. In Christ's name, we pray. Amen*

Thought for the day: What gift can I use to glorify God?

Nancy C. Todd (Kentucky, US)

FRIDAY 26 AUGUST

In the Fog

Read Luke 24:13–35

'What no eye has seen, what no ear has heard, and what no human mind has conceived'—the things God has prepared for those who love him.
1 Corinthians 2:9 (NIV)

I left work early and decided to take a scenic route home. I normally saw rolling hills, vibrant colourful fields and horses grazing by the roadside. But that day all I could see was mist, rain and fog. I felt as if I was driving into nothing. The drive home echoed my life at that time. I had just received a letter warning me that my job was at risk. A timeline of what would happen next had been explained to me, but my future was uncertain. I was going into a foggy time in life and had to trust God for direction.

A few months later, I drove the same route again. The sun illuminated the scenery I remembered and I could see all around. Once again, these surroundings mirrored how I felt about my life. I had a new job and God's direction for my life had become clear. The Lord led me through the fog back into the light and the beauty of life once more.

We all face times of uncertainty when the road ahead is not clear. We often cannot comprehend why it is happening or where we will end up. Just as the two disciples walking to Emmaus recognised Jesus, sometimes our eyes are suddenly opened and we understand God's purpose and direction. Even when we are not aware, God is always with us.

Prayer: *Faithful God, help us to trust your guidance even when we can't see the path ahead. Amen*

Thought for the day: When the path forward is unclear, I can trust God for direction.

Chris Hall (Berkshire, England)

PRAYER FOCUS: SOMEONE WHO HAS LOST A JOB

SATURDAY 27 AUGUST

Depth of Devotion

Read Mark 1:16–20

At that very moment [Jesus] called them. They followed him, leaving their father Zebedee in the boat with the hired workers.
Mark 1:20 (CEB)

When Jesus called his disciples, they were already settled into their jobs. From today's reading, it appears that they were having successful careers. But the call of Christ and a new way of life took precedence. Their allegiance was total or a 'whole devotion', without hesitation or regret, to the cause to which Christ called them.

As Christians we can be devoted to many things. Our families, our church, our jobs, our education, our reputation and other aspects of our life beckon us. All of them need our attention. But as the disciples demonstrated, our devotion to Christ is our first and primary allegiance. We are called by Christ to be devoted witnesses of our faith. The disciples exemplified such devotion, and so can we.

Prayer: *Dear Lord, help us to be faithful to you. Search us and call us back to you when we fall short. Strengthen us to be wholehearted in our devotion to you. Amen*

Thought for the day: When Christ calls, I will follow.

William L. Dike (Maryland, US)

SUNDAY 28 AUGUST

Trust God

Read Psalm 106:24–27

Be strong and courageous. Do not be afraid; do not be discouraged, for the Lord your God will be with you wherever you go.
Joshua 1:9 (NIV)

The phone call from my local college inviting me to teach plunged me into panic. I thought about all the potential problems. What if I don't know enough about the material? What if the students ask questions I can't answer? What if they realise I don't know everything? I was faced with a choice: would I succumb to fear or trust the promise in Philippians 4:13 that I can do all things with God's help?

As I thought about my options, I remembered the Israelites who stood outside the promised land filled with fear. They didn't believe God's promise of success. They worried about the giants in the land. They forgot all the wonderful miracles God did to bring them out of Egypt.

I decided the best option was to trust God despite my fear and to accept the teaching offer. Despite all the unknowns, I clung to God's promise to be with me. He gave me the strength, knowledge and perseverance to guide the class. When we are faced with a new challenge, we can remember God's past faithfulness. These memories provide the courage to accept each new challenge that comes our way.

Prayer: *Dear God, thank you for being with us on our journey. Help us through the challenges we face. Amen*

Thought for the day: God helps me to face each new challenge.

Lynn Karidis (Michigan, US)

PRAYER FOCUS: NEW TEACHERS

MONDAY 29 AUGUST

Praying for Patience

Read Isaiah 40:27–31
The fruit of the Spirit is love, joy, peace, patience, kindness, generosity, faithfulness, gentleness, and self-control.
Galatians 5:22–23 (NRSV)

After thyroid surgery I was not able to speak above a whisper. Although my surgeon was concerned, he assured me that my voice should return to normal in about six weeks.

I was worried. What was I to do about my preaching responsibilities if my voice was not restored? Would I have to leave the pastoral ministry? Would I lose my voice completely?

I prayed for healing, but I soon realised that I also had to pray for patience. I asked God to teach me how to wait. And while I waited, I resumed my Sunday preaching schedule carefully, with some reservation.

After about six weeks, I was talking in a whisper on the telephone when my voice regained its normal resonance. Since then, my voice has never wavered in strength and quality—and I am amazed by God's comforting presence. He taught me how to wait with abundant hope and enabled me to engage in ministry with new strength and energy.

Prayer: *Dear God, as we rush through life, slow us down. Teach us how to wait with patience and hope. Amen*

Thought for the day: Today I will look for patience in the presence of God.

Ernest S. Lyght (New Jersey, US)

PRAYER FOCUS: SOMEONE WHO STRUGGLES TO BE PATIENT

TUESDAY 30 AUGUST

Deeper Understanding

Read Matthew 13:1–9

If my people would only listen to me, if Israel would only follow my ways, how quickly I would subdue their enemies and turn my hand against their foes!
Psalm 81:13–14 (NIV)

As a tutor, I like to observe my students' diligence and seriousness in learning. Each student has textbooks, a teacher and all they need to learn, but only some of them are actually using what they have to deepen their understanding.

Similarly, in our Christian lives, we have the Bible, spiritual leaders and mentors and fellowship with other Christians to help us grow in our faith. However, not all of us pursue spiritual growth with the same passion. If we are close to God and always pray, read and meditate on his word, we can deepen our understanding and our faith. When we face trials, the peace of the Lord can sustain us. We will be like seeds that fall on good soil and bring forth grain. We will yield a crop 30, 60, a hundredfold for the kingdom of God.

Prayer: *Dear God, help us to draw close to you through your word as we pray, 'Our Father which art in heaven, Hallowed be thy name. Thy kingdom come. Thy will be done in earth, as it is in heaven. Give us this day our daily bread. And forgive us our debts, as we forgive our debtors. And lead us not into temptation, but deliver us from evil: For thine is the kingdom, and the power, and the glory, for ever.'* Amen*

Thought for the day: How can I use what I have to deepen my faith?

Linawati Santoso (East Java, Indonesia)

PRAYER FOCUS: STUDENTS
* Matthew 6:9–13 (KJV)

WEDNESDAY 31 AUGUST

When We are Overwhelmed

Read 1 Peter 5:5–7

When you pass through the waters, I will be with you; and through the rivers, they shall not overwhelm you.
Isaiah 43:2 (NRSV)

Sometimes I am overwhelmed—by too much change in a short amount of time or too many projects half done or too many conflicts unresolved. I've found that when I get truly overwhelmed I can get to the point of not doing much of anything because I am unable to do everything.

In a church where I was the minister many years ago, I felt overwhelmed. A good friend noticed, took me aside and said, 'This church didn't become like this in a month or a year. You can't do everything, especially straight away. Do what you can and give the rest a nod and a prayer.'

At first, I thought perhaps this advice did not take the situation seriously, but the more I thought on it, the better I understood. To give overwhelming situations a nod and a prayer was and is fitting advice. A nod indicates that we see the problem; we are not turning a blind eye to it or ignoring it. That problem will just have to wait its turn. A prayer says that for the moment we are leaving it in the hands of God. Perhaps God has another servant equipped and better prepared for the challenge. With a nod and a prayer, we allow ourselves and others to answer God's call to do the work set before us.

Prayer: *Dear Lord, thank you for helping us when we feel overwhelmed. Help us to remember that not every task is ours alone to complete. Amen*

Thought for the day: What is God calling me to let go of today?

Michael Sanders (Michigan, US)

Small Group Questions

Wednesday 4 May

1. Describe your prayer life. How often do you pray? What form do your prayers most often take? What challenges do you face in your prayer life?

2. Have you ever had a prayer answered in an unexpected way? What was that experience like?

3. When and where did you learn how to pray? Has the way in which you pray changed over the course of your life? If so, how?

4. Are there any specific prayer practices to which you are drawn or that have been particularly helpful to you, such as lectio divina or contemplative prayer? What is it about these specific prayer practices that appeals to you?

5. Is waiting easy or difficult for you? Do you identify with the challenge Sue describes of waiting for a prayer to be answered?

Wednesday 11 May

1. Can you recall a time when you have forgiven someone who harmed you in some way? What was that experience like for you?

2. Can you recall a time when someone has forgiven you for a harm you caused? Describe that experience.

3. What stories in the Bible can you think of that relate to forgiveness? How do you connect with these stories?

4. What challenges are there in forgiving someone? Why is forgiveness important?

5. How does your faith community model forgiveness? How does your community support those who are struggling to forgive or who ask for forgiveness?

Wednesday 18 May

1. Recall a time when someone has said something to you that has given you encouragement or strength. What was going on in your life at the time? What did the person say?

2. Ramona quotes Psalm 19:14: 'Let the words of my mouth and the meditation of my heart be acceptable to you, O Lord, my rock and my redeemer.' What does this verse mean to you? How can you put this verse into action in your daily life?

3. Can you think of a time when someone has spoken words to you that were unhelpful or hurtful, even though the person had good intentions? What was the experience like for you?

4. Can you think of a time when you have spoken words to someone that proved unhelpful or hurtful, even though your intentions were good? What did you learn from the situation? What might you have done that was different?

5. What other scripture passages relate to the words that we speak? How does scripture help you to consider the way you speak to others?

Wednesday 25 May

1. Is making decisions easy or difficult for you? When faced with a big decision, how do you approach it? Seek the advice of family, friends, or colleagues? Step back, take a look at the big picture and go from there? Some combination of these?

2. What role does prayer play in your decision-making? Are there other spiritual practices you use when faced with a big decision?

3. Was there ever a time in your life when you were really lost? What got you back on the right path?

4. Jerry writes, 'Our world can offer any number of tempting paths, which may or may not prove to be the right direction for us.' How do you relate to this statement? Can you describe a time in your life when you started down one path only to discover it was not the right direction for you?

5. Are there ways in which your life might have been different had you chosen other paths?

Wednesday 1 June

1. Denise mentions the saying, 'God will not give you more than you can handle.' Do you agree with her that statements such as these 'often cannot provide the comfort one hopes to receive when going through a difficult situation'? Why or why not?

2. What other statements do you hear people make to those experiencing difficult times? Can you think of reasons why such statements may be more damaging than helpful?

3. What does it mean to you that even Paul experienced trials that he admitted were more than he could handle?

4. In what ways does your community of faith support those going through hard times?

5. Who in your community of faith needs prayers of support today? How will you pray for them? Will you let them know of your prayers? How?

Wednesday 8 June

1. What do you think of Chad's experience with Frank? Have you had any similar experiences, when after getting to know someone you realise he or she is different from what you first thought?

2. Can you name people or groups in our society who are often overlooked or misjudged? Who in your community is often overlooked or misjudged? Why do you think this is?

3. How would the world be different if we recognised others by their 'fruit' and not their appearance? What might be challenging about this?

4. Can you think of an example from the Bible in which a person was judged solely by his or her outward appearance? What can we learn from this?

5. What ministries does your church or community have that reach out to those who are homeless? What are some ways that you can get involved?

Wednesday 15 June

1. Is Marie's response to her circumstances simple or challenging for you to understand? Why?

2. Recall a time when you responded to a situation with love and compassion instead of anger. What was this like for you? What was the outcome?

3. Can you think of an instance in which you responded to a situation out of anger instead of love and compassion? Looking back, how might you have approached the situation differently?

4. Jean, the writer of today's meditation, quotes Proverbs 17:9. What does this verse mean to you?

5. To whom in your life do you need to show the most love and compassion today? What would this cost you? How would it benefit you?

Wednesday 22 June

1. Do you remember what it was like to be a new believer? Describe that time in your life.

2. What does it mean to accept 'new believers where they are on their Christian journeys'? Do you agree that this is the best approach?

3. Name some of the people who have influenced you on your Christian journey. In what ways did they encourage, nurture and support you?

4. What insights have you gained on your journey that you would want to offer new believers?

5. Who are the new believers in your community of faith? What can you do to help them on their journey?

Wednesday 29 June

1. Spiritually speaking, how do you relate to David's story?

2. How do you think the disciples in Luke 5 felt after fishing all night and catching nothing, only to throw their nets to the other side and have them become full?

3. David writes, 'Learning how to be a disciple requires persistence, good practice and a sense of peace.' Can you think of other qualities that come with learning how to be a disciple?

4. Name some of the ways in which you serve Jesus Christ. What sense of purpose do you derive from this service?

5. What would you say to someone who has felt spiritually ineffective for a long time? What Bible verses might you point them to? What words of encouragement from your own experience might you offer them?

Wednesday 6 July

1. How did your childhood shape your understanding of God? How did you relate to him as a child? Who taught you about him?

2. If you could speak to your childhood self, what would you want to say about faith and about God? How might you share this wisdom with other young people?

3. Recall a time when God was faithful to you. Describe your situation. How did you recognise God's presence?

4. Kathleen writes, 'Trusting God is one thing; faithfulness to God is another.' Do you agree or disagree with this statement? How are trust and faith different for you? How are they similar?

5. How does your church help you to remember and recognise God's faithfulness? What rituals, prayers or practices help the congregation and the community feel God's presence and trust him more deeply?

Wednesday 13 July

1. When have you been asked to assist with a project you felt ill-equipped to help with? Did you participate or not? How did you feel about your decision?

2. Have you ever invited someone to participate in a project or event, knowing that he or she may not be perfectly suited to the activity? If so, why did you invite that person? What did you hope the outcome would be?

3. Name some biblical figures who felt unprepared for the tasks to which God called them. Which of these figures can you most closely relate to?

4. Faith's story demonstrates hospitality on the part of the skilled workers; they found meaningful work for her to do, despite her lack of experience. Where have you witnessed similar acts of hospitality in your community?

5. How does your church validate and employ the diverse talents and gifts of the members of the congregation? In what other ways might you encourage your church to help people find meaningful roles in the community?

Wednesday 20 July

1. Describe your regular devotional practice. What do you like about Marney's practice? What new practice would you like to try?

2. How do you make note of or remember God's presence with you during difficult times? How does reflecting on God's past faithfulness help you to have hope for the future?

3. What passages of scripture do you turn to in times of stress? Joy? Frustration? Confusion? Hope?

4. How does your church interact with scripture during worship? Is it the central focus of the service? The supporting text for the sermon, music and ritual?

5. Think of a time when a Bible verse has comforted or guided you differently in different situations. What was the verse, and how did it guide you in each situation?

Wednesday 27 July

1. What was your first reaction to Paul's story in today's meditation? Could you relate to his experience? Why or why not?

2. When Paul says his mother's faith 'led her to look ahead with spiritual excitement' what do you think he means?

3. Recall a time when you were 'having fun' living your faith. What were you doing? Who was with you? Why was it fun? How might you bring some of that fun into your faith life today?

4. How can the faith of Paul's mother help you think about death in a new way? What insight does Paul's mother offer you?

5. What scripture passages comfort you in times of mourning? What passages help you to think about eternal life?

Wednesday 3 August

1. Recall a time when you encountered strangers or immigrants in your community. What was this encounter like for you?

2. With whom have your shared your faith recently? Did you begin the conversation, or did someone ask you about your faith? How did this conversation make you feel?

3. Read Genesis 18:1–10. How is this story a model of hospitality? How might you follow this example in your own life?

4. What opportunities for spiritual growth do you see in getting to know someone who speaks a different language and has different customs from yourself?

5. How does your church welcome newcomers to worship services or to the community? In what ways can your church become more welcoming?

Wednesday 10 August

1. What is your favourite Bible verse or story? When did it become your favourite? Why is it your favourite?

2. Do you know someone whose life is 'rooted in scripture'? What does this person do or say to show you that scripture is a deep part of his or her life of faith?

3. What Bible verses have you memorised? Do you enjoy memorising scripture? How do you think memorising scripture helps someone to understand or engage with the Bible differently from simply reading it?

4. How would you describe the difference between God's success and prosperity and worldly success and prosperity? How can you seek God's success and prosperity in your daily life?

5. Is there a Bible verse or story that is empowering you to do something today? If so, what is the verse or story, and what is it urging you to do?

Wednesday 17 August

1. Imagine you are the widow in Mark 12:41–44. What worries or concerns do you have? What are you thinking as you give your coins to the treasury? What do you hope the crowd of onlookers will say or do as you walk by?

2. Now imagine you are among the disciples. What are you thinking? How do Jesus' words change your thinking about the widow's offering? What do you want to say to the widow?

3. Recall a time when you gave a generous gift. Did giving this gift feel like a sacrifice on your part? How did the receiver respond to your gift? How did others who knew about the gift react?

4. Can you think of a time when someone has given you a gift that you knew represented a great sacrifice from the giver? What was this experience like for you?

5. How does your church acknowledge gifts of time, talents or money? Are gifts received gratefully regardless of their size or extravagance? How might your church receive and acknowledge gifts more graciously?

Wednesday 24 August

1. How do you relate to Sharon's story? Have you ever visited or befriended someone who is in prison? What was the experience like for you?

2. Sharon writes, 'If we are honest, we can all admit to having some form of confinement that threatens our peace.' How does this statement resonate with you?

3. What is confining you? Stress? Family obligations? Work? Illness?

4. When has your faith been enriched by a friendship? How did this friendship begin? What did this person help you to learn or understand about faith?

5. What spiritual practices help you to remember the freedom God offers? What new practice would you like to try?

Wednesday 31 August

1. Describe a time when you felt overwhelmed. What caused this feeling? How did you cope with it?

2. Do you find Michael's practice for dealing with overwhelming situations helpful? Why or why not?

3. Whom do you turn to in times of stress or anxiety? Why do you turn to this person?

4. What stories from scripture help you when you feel overwhelmed? How do these passages give you comfort, courage, or strength?

5. How does your faith community help people to care for themselves in times of stress? How does your community encourage others to make their needs known? In what other ways could your community be supportive in helping people deal with overwhelming situations?

Journal page

Journal page

Journal page

Journal page

Journal page

Journal page

Journal page

NEW FROM BRF

Messy Hospitality

Changing communities through fun, food, friendship and faith

Lucy Moore

In *Messy Hospitality* Lucy Moore demonstrates how hospitality can be practised in Messy Church and other church contexts to promote mission and faith formation, addressing the theology of hospitality and how it can be expressed at the welcome table, the activity table, the Lord's Table, the meal table, and in the home.

Also included are insights from the secular hospitality industry, how to train Messy Church teams in hospitality, audit-style questions for the reader to apply in their own context, and five complete session outlines for Messy Churches.

ISBN 978 0 85746 415 6 £9.99
To order a copy of this book, please turn to the order form on page 159.

NEW FROM BRF

Heaven's Morning

Rethinking the destination

David Winter

The Bible—especially the New Testament—has plenty to say about resurrection and heaven, but many Christians struggle to make sense of what it actually means in practice. David Winter's accessible book explores the biblical teaching on what happens after death and considers what difference this can make to our lives here and now. He also shows how we can present what we believe about eternity as a source of hope to our sceptical, anxious world.

ISBN 978 0 85746 476 7 £7.99
To order a copy of this book, please turn to the order form on page 159.

NEW FROM BRF

St Aidan's Way of Mission

Celtic insights for a post-Christian world

Ray Simpson with Brent Lyons-Lee

Surveying the life and times of Aidan of Lindisfarne, this book draws insights into missional approaches to inspire both outreach and discipleship for today's church. As in his previous BRF book, *Hilda of Whitby*, Ray Simpson shows that such figures from past centuries can provide models for Christian life and witness today. An author and speaker on Celtic spirituality with a worldwide reputation, he combines historical fact with spiritual lessons in a highly accessible style.

ISBN 978 0 85746 485 9   £7.99
To order a copy of this book, please turn to the order form on page 159.

ALSO FROM BRF

Confidence in the Living God

David and Goliath revisited

Andrew Watson

Confidence lies at the heart of society, determining the success or failure of the economy, the government, companies, schools, churches and individuals. As Christians, we are called to proclaim our faith in God, but how can we build and maintain this confidence in an increasingly secularised culture where such faith is often seen as marginal, embarrassing or even downright dangerous?

Using the story of David and Goliath as his starting-point, Andrew Watson shows how the Lord can indeed be our confidence, whatever the odds. He explores how God can develop a proper self-confidence within individuals and his church, revealing the gospel through transforming words and transformed lives. He considers, too, how we can confidently tackle the challenges of day-to-day living, whether a difficult work situation or family relationship, or simply anxiety about the future. The book includes a discussion guide and is ideal as a whole church course on the subject of confidence.

ISBN 978 0 85746 482 8   £7.99
To order a copy of this book, please turn to the order form on page 159.

How to encourage Bible reading in your church

BRF has been helping individuals connect with the Bible for over 90 years. We want to support churches as they seek to encourage church members into regular Bible reading.

Order a Bible reading resources pack
This pack is designed to give your church the tools to publicise our Bible reading notes. It includes:

- Sample Bible reading notes for your congregation to try.
- Publicity resources, including a poster.
- A church magazine feature about Bible reading notes.

The pack is free, but we welcome a £5 donation to cover the cost of postage. If you require a pack to be sent outside the UK or require a specific number of sample Bible reading notes, please contact us for postage costs. More information about what the current pack contains is available on our website.

How to order and find out more
- Visit **www.biblereadingnotes.org.uk/for-churches/**
- Telephone BRF on 01865 319700 between 9.15 am and 5.30 pm.
- Write to us at BRF, 15 The Chambers, Vineyard, Abingdon, OX14 3FE.

Keep informed about our latest initiatives
We are continuing to develop resources to help churches encourage people into regular Bible reading, wherever they are on their journey. Join our email list at **www.biblereadingnotes.org.uk/helpingchurches/** to stay informed about the latest initiatives that your church could benefit from.

Introduce a friend to our notes
We can send information about our notes and current prices for you to pass on. Please contact us.

BRF is a Registered Charity

Subscriptions

The Upper Room is published in January, May and September.

Individual subscriptions

The subscription rate for orders for 4 or fewer copies includes postage and packing: THE UPPER ROOM annual individual subscription £16.20

Church subscriptions

Orders for 5 copies or more, sent to ONE address, are post free:
THE UPPER ROOM annual church subscription £13.05

Please do not send payment with order for a church subscription. We will send an invoice with your first order.

Please note that the annual billing period for church subscriptions runs from 1 May to 30 April.

Copies of the notes may also be obtained from Christian bookshops.

Single copies of *The Upper Room* will cost £4.35. Prices valid until 30 April 2017.

Giant print version

The Upper Room is available in giant print for the visually impaired, from:

Torch Trust for the Blind
Torch House
Torch Way,
Northampton Road
Market Harborough
LE16 9HL

Tel: 01858 438260
www.torchtrust.org

Individual Subscriptions

☐ I would like to take out a subscription myself (complete your name and address details only once)

☐ I would like to give a gift subscription (please complete both name and address sections below)

Your name..

Your address...

....Postcode...

Your telephone number..

Gift subscription name..

Gift subscription address..

....Postcode...

Gift message (20 words max)...

....

Please send *The Upper Room* beginning with the September 2016 / January 2017 / May 2017 issue: (delete as applicable)

THE UPPER ROOM ☐ £16.20

Please complete the payment details below and send, with appropriate payment, to: BRF, 15 The Chambers, Vineyard, Abingdon OX14 3FE

Total enclosed £ .... (cheques should be made payable to 'BRF')

Payment by ☐ cheque ☐ postal order ☐ Visa ☐ Mastercard ☐ Switch

Card no: │

Expires: │ │ │ │   Security code: │ │ │ │

Issue no (Switch): │ │ │ │

Signature (essential if paying by credit/Switch card) ....

☐ Please do not send me further information about BRF publications

☐ Please send me a Bible reading resources pack to encourage Bible reading in my church

BRF is a Registered Charity

Church Subscriptions

☐ Please send me ... copies of *The Upper Room* September 2016 / January 2017 / May 2017 issue (delete as applicable)

Name..

Address ....

....Postcode..

Telephone ....

Email..

Please send this completed form to:
BRF, 15 The Chambers, Vineyard, Abingdon OX14 3FE

Please do not send payment with this order. We will send an invoice with your first order.

Christian bookshops: All good Christian bookshops stock BRF publications. For your nearest stockist, please contact BRF.

Telephone: The BRF office is open between 09.15 and 17.30. To place your order, telephone 01865 319700; fax 01865 319701.

Web: Visit www.brf.org.uk

☐ Please send me a Bible reading resources pack to encourage Bible reading in my church

BRF is a Registered Charity

ORDER FORM				
REF	TITLE	PRICE	QTY	TOTAL
415 6	Messy Hospitality	£9.99		
476 7	Heaven's Morning	£7.99		
485 9	St Aidan's Way of Mission	£7.99		
482 8	Confidence in the Living God	£7.99		

Postage and packing
Donation
TOTAL

POSTAGE AND PACKING CHARGES				
Order value	UK	Europe	Economy (Surface)	Standard (Air)
Under £7.00	£1.25	£3.00	£3.50	£5.50
£7.00–£29.99	£2.25	£5.50	£6.50	£10.00
£30.00 and over	FREE	prices on request		

Name _____ Account Number _____

Address _____

_____ Postcode _____

Telephone Number _____

Email _____

Payment by: ❏ Cheque ❏ Mastercard ❏ Visa ❏ Postal Order ❏ Maestro

Card no ☐☐☐☐ ☐☐☐☐ ☐☐☐☐ ☐☐☐☐ ☐☐☐

Valid from ☐☐☐☐ Expires ☐☐☐☐ Issue no. ☐☐☐

Security code* ☐☐☐

*Last 3 digits on the reverse of the card.
ESSENTIAL IN ORDER TO PROCESS YOUR ORDER

Shaded boxes for Maestro use only

Signature _____ Date _____

All orders must be accompanied by the appropriate payment.

Please send your completed order form to:
BRF, 15 The Chambers, Vineyard, Abingdon OX14 3FE
Tel. 01865 319700 / Fax. 01865 319701 Email: enquiries@brf.org.uk

❏ Please send me further information about BRF publications.

Available from your local Christian bookshop.   BRF is a Registered Charity